Regular Expression
Pocket Reference

D1510243

SECOND EDITION

Regular Expression
Pocket Reference

Tony Stubblebine

O'REILLY®

Beijing · Cambridge · Farnham · Köln · Sebastopol · Tokyo

Regular Expression Pocket Reference, Second Edition

by Tony Stubblebine

Printed in the United States of America.

Published by O'Reilly Media, Inc., 1005 Gravenstein Highway North, Sebastopol, CA 95472.

O'Reilly books may be purchased for educational, business, or sales promotional use. Online editions are also available for most titles (*safari.oreilly.com*). For more information, contact our corporate/institutional sales department: (800) 998-9938 or *corporate@oreilly.com*.

Editor: Andy Oram	**Indexer:** Johnna VanHoose Dinse
Production Editor: Sumita Mukherji	**Cover Designer:** Karen Montgomery
Copyeditor: Genevieve d'Entremont	**Interior Designer:** David Futato

Printing History:

August 2003:	First Edition.
July 2007:	Second Edition.

ISBN: 978-0-596-51427-3
[LSI]   [2011-06-24]

Contents

Regular Expression Pocket Reference

Regular expressions are a language used for parsing and manipulating text. They are often used to perform complex search-and-replace operations, and to validate that text data is well-formed.

Today, regular expressions are included in most programming languages, as well as in many scripting languages, editors, applications, databases, and command-line tools. This book aims to give quick access to the syntax and pattern-matching operations of the most popular of these languages so that you can apply your regular-expression knowledge in any environment.

The second edition of this book adds sections on Ruby and Apache web server, common regular expressions, and also updates existing languages.

About This Book

This book starts with a general introduction to regular expressions. The first section describes and defines the constructs used in regular expressions, and establishes the common principles of pattern matching. The remaining sections of the book are devoted to the syntax, features, and usage of regular expressions in various implementations.

The implementations covered in this book are Perl, Java™, .NET and C#, Ruby, Python, PCRE, PHP, Apache web server, *vi* editor, JavaScript, and shell tools.

Conventions Used in This Book

The following typographical conventions are used in this book:

Italic
> Used for emphasis, new terms, program names, and URLs

Constant width
> Used for options, values, code fragments, and any text that should be typed literally

Constant width italic
> Used for text that should be replaced with user-supplied values

Constant width bold
> Used in examples for commands or other text that should be typed literally by the user

Acknowledgments

Jeffrey E. F. Friedl's *Mastering Regular Expressions* (O'Reilly) is the definitive work on regular expressions. While writing, I relied heavily on his book and his advice. As a convenience, this book provides page references to *Mastering Regular Expressions*, Third Edition (MRE) for expanded discussion of regular expression syntax and concepts.

Nat Torkington and Linda Mui were excellent editors who guided me through what turned out to be a tricky first edition. This edition was aided by the excellent editorial skills of Andy Oram. Sarah Burcham deserves special thanks for giving me the opportunity to write this book, and for her contributions to the "Shell Tools" section. More thanks for the input and technical reviews from Jeffrey Friedl, Philip Hazel, Steve Friedl, Ola Bini, Ian Darwin, Zak Greant, Ron Hitchens, A.M. Kuchling, Tim Allwine, Schuyler Erle, David Lents, Rabble, Rich Bowan, Eric Eisenhart, and Brad Merrill.

Introduction to Regexes and Pattern Matching

A *regular expression* is a string containing a combination of normal characters and special metacharacters or metasequences. The normal characters match themselves. *Metacharacters* and *metasequences* are characters or sequences of characters that represent ideas such as quantity, locations, or types of characters. The list in "Regex Metacharacters, Modes, and Constructs" shows the most common metacharacters and metasequences in the regular expression world. Later sections list the availability of and syntax for supported metacharacters for particular implementations of regular expressions.

Pattern matching consists of finding a section of text that is described (matched) by a regular expression. The underlying code that searches the text is the *regular expression engine*. You can predict the results of most matches by keeping two rules in mind:

1. The earliest (leftmost) match wins

   Regular expressions are applied to the input starting at the first character and proceeding toward the last. As soon as the regular expression engine finds a match, it returns. (See MRE 148–149.)

2. Standard quantifiers are greedy

   Quantifiers specify how many times something can be repeated. The standard quantifiers attempt to match as many times as possible. They settle for less than the maximum only if this is necessary for the success of the match. The process of giving up characters and trying less-greedy matches is called backtracking. (See MRE 151–153.)

Regular expression engines have differences based on their type. There are two classes of engines: Deterministic Finite Automaton (DFA) and Nondeterministic Finite Automaton

(NFA). DFAs are faster, but lack many of the features of an NFA, such as capturing, lookaround, and nongreedy quantifiers. In the NFA world, there are two types: traditional and POSIX.

DFA engines

DFAs compare each character of the input string to the regular expression, keeping track of all matches in progress. Since each character is examined at most once, the DFA engine is the fastest. One additional rule to remember with DFAs is that the alternation metasequence is greedy. When more than one option in an alternation (foo|foobar) matches, the longest one is selected. So, rule No. 1 can be amended to read "the longest leftmost match wins." (See MRE 155–156.)

Traditional NFA engines

Traditional NFA engines compare each element of the regex to the input string, keeping track of positions where it chose between two options in the regex. If an option fails, the engine backtracks to the most recently saved position. For standard quantifiers, the engine chooses the greedy option of matching more text; however, if that option leads to the failure of the match, the engine returns to a saved position and tries a less greedy path. The traditional NFA engine uses ordered alternation, where each option in the alternation is tried sequentially. A longer match may be ignored if an earlier option leads to a successful match. So, here rule #1 can be amended to read "the first leftmost match after greedy quantifiers have had their fill wins." (See MRE 153–154.)

POSIX NFA engines

POSIX NFA Engines work similarly to Traditional NFAs with one exception: a POSIX engine always picks the longest of the leftmost matches. For example, the alternation cat|category would match the full word "category" whenever possible, even if the first alternative ("cat") matched and appeared earlier in the alternation. (See MRE 153–154.)

Regex Metacharacters, Modes, and Constructs

The metacharacters and metasequences shown here represent most available types of regular expression constructs and their most common syntax. However, syntax and availability vary by implementation.

Character representations

Many implementations provide shortcuts to represent characters that may be difficult to input. (See MRE 115–118.)

Character shorthands
> Most implementations have specific shorthands for the alert, backspace, escape character, form feed, newline, carriage return, horizontal tab, and vertical tab characters. For example, \n is often a shorthand for the newline character, which is usually LF (012 octal), but can sometimes be CR (015 octal), depending on the operating system. Confusingly, many implementations use \b to mean both backspace and word boundary (position between a "word" character and a nonword character). For these implementations, \b means backspace in a character class (a set of possible characters to match in the string), and word boundary elsewhere.

Octal escape: \num
> Represents a character corresponding to a two- or three-digit octal number. For example, \015\012 matches an ASCII CR/LF sequence.

Hex and Unicode escapes: \xnum, \x{num}, \unum, \Unum
> Represent characters corresponding to hexadecimal numbers. Four-digit and larger hex numbers can represent the range of Unicode characters. For example, \x0D\x0A matches an ASCII CR/LF sequence.

Control characters: \cchar
> Corresponds to ASCII control characters encoded with values less than 32. To be safe, always use an uppercase *char*—some implementations do not handle lowercase

representations. For example, \cH matches Control-H, an
ASCII backspace character.

Character classes and class-like constructs

Character classes are used to specify a set of characters. A character class matches a single character in the input string that is within the defined set of characters. (See MRE 118–128.)

Normal classes: [...] *and* [^...]

> Character classes, [...], and negated character classes,
> [^...], allow you to list the characters that you do or do
> not want to match. A character class always matches one
> character. The - (dash) indicates a range of characters.
> For example, [a-z] matches any lowercase ASCII letter.
> To include the dash in the list of characters, either list it
> first, or escape it.

Almost any character: dot (.)

> Usually matches any character except a newline. However, the match mode usually can be changed so that dot
> also matches newlines. Inside a character class, dot
> matches just a dot.

Class shorthands: \w, \d, \s, \W, \D, \S

> Commonly provided shorthands for word character,
> digit, and space character classes. A word character is
> often all ASCII alphanumeric characters plus the underscore. However, the list of alphanumerics can include
> additional locale or Unicode alphanumerics, depending
> on the implementation. A lowercase shorthand (e.g., \s)
> matches a character from the class; uppercase (e.g., \S)
> matches a character not from the class. For example, \d
> matches a single digit character, and is usually equivalent to [0-9].

POSIX character class: [:alnum:]

> POSIX defines several character classes that can be used
> only within regular expression character classes (see
> Table 1). Take, for example, [:lower:]. When written as
> [[:lower:]], it is equivalent to [a-z] in the ASCII locale.

Table 1. POSIX character classes

Class	Meaning
Alnum	Letters and digits.
Alpha	Letters.
Blank	Space or tab only.
Cntrl	Control characters.
Digit	Decimal digits.
Graph	Printing characters, excluding space.
Lower	Lowercase letters.
Print	Printing characters, including space.
Punct	Printing characters, excluding letters and digits.
Space	Whitespace.
Upper	Uppercase letters.
Xdigit	Hexadecimal digits.

Unicode properties, scripts, and blocks: \p{*prop*}, \P{*prop*}

> The Unicode standard defines classes of characters that have a particular property, belong to a script, or exist within a block. *Properties* are the character's defining characteristics, such as being a letter or a number (see Table 2). *Scripts* are systems of writing, such as Hebrew, Latin, or Han. *Blocks* are ranges of characters on the Unicode character map. Some implementations require that Unicode properties be prefixed with Is or In. For example, \p{Ll} matches lowercase letters in any Unicode-supported language, such as a or α.

Unicode combining character sequence: \X

> Matches a Unicode base character followed by any number of Unicode-combining characters. This is a shorthand for \P{M}\p{M}. For example, \X matches è; as well as the two characters e'.

Table 2. Standard Unicode properties

Property	Meaning
\p{L}	Letters.
\p{Ll}	Lowercase letters.
\p{Lm}	Modifier letters.
\p{Lo}	Letters, other. These have no case, and are not considered modifiers.
\p{Lt}	Titlecase letters.
\p{Lu}	Uppercase letters.
\p{C}	Control codes and characters not in other categories.
\p{Cc}	ASCII and Latin-1 control characters.
\p{Cf}	Nonvisible formatting characters.
\p{Cn}	Unassigned code points.
\p{Co}	Private use, such as company logos.
\p{Cs}	Surrogates.
\p{M}	Marks meant to combine with base characters, such as accent marks.
\p{Mc}	Modification characters that take up their own space. Examples include "vowel signs."
\p{Me}	Marks that enclose other characters, such as circles, squares, and diamonds.
\p{Mn}	Characters that modify other characters, such as accents and umlauts.
\p{N}	Numeric characters.
\p{Nd}	Decimal digits in various scripts.
\p{Nl}	Letters that represent numbers, such as Roman numerals.
\p{No}	Superscripts, symbols, or nondigit characters representing numbers.
\p{P}	Punctuation.
\p{Pc}	Connecting punctuation, such as an underscore.
\p{Pd}	Dashes and hyphens.
\p{Pe}	Closing punctuation complementing \p{Ps}.
\p{Pi}	Initial punctuation, such as opening quotes.

Table 2. Standard Unicode properties (continued)

Property	Meaning
\p{Pf}	Final punctuation, such as closing quotes.
\p{Po}	Other punctuation marks.
\p{Ps}	Opening punctuation, such as opening parentheses.
\p{S}	Symbols.
\p{Sc}	Currency.
\p{Sk}	Combining characters represented as individual characters.
\p{Sm}	Math symbols.
\p{So}	Other symbols.
\p{Z}	Separating characters with no visual representation.
\p{Zl}	Line separators.
\p{Zp}	Paragraph separators.
\p{Zs}	Space characters.

Anchors and zero-width assertions

Anchors and "zero-width assertions" match positions in the input string. (See MRE 128–134.)

Start of line/string: ^, \A
> Matches at the beginning of the text being searched. In multiline mode, ^ matches after any newline. Some implementations support \A, which matches only at the beginning of the text.

End of line/string: $, \Z, \z
> $ matches at the end of a string. In multiline mode, $ matches before any newline. When supported, \Z matches the end of string or the point before a string-ending newline, regardless of match mode. Some implementations also provide \z, which matches only the end of the string, regardless of newlines.

Start of match: \G

> In iterative matching, \G matches the position where the previous match ended. Often, this spot is reset to the beginning of a string on a failed match.

Word boundary: \b, \B, \<, \>

> Word boundary metacharacters match a location where a word character is next to a nonword character. \b often specifies a word boundary location, and \B often specifies a not-word-boundary location. Some implementations provide separate metasequences for start- and end-of-word boundaries, often \< and \>.

Lookahead: (?=...), (?!...)
Lookbehind: (?<=...), (?<!...)

> *Lookaround constructs* match a location in the text where the subpattern would match (lookahead), would not match (negative lookahead), would have finished matching (lookbehind), or would not have finished matching (negative lookbehind). For example, foo(?=bar) matches foo in foobar, but not food. Implementations often limit lookbehind constructs to subpatterns with a predetermined length.

Comments and mode modifiers

Mode modifiers change how the regular expression engine interprets a regular expression. (See MRE 110–113, 135–136.)

Multiline mode: m

> Changes the behavior of ^ and $ to match next to newlines within the input string.

Single-line mode: s

> Changes the behavior of . (dot) to match all characters, including newlines, within the input string.

Case-insensitive mode: i

> Treat letters that differ only in case as identical.

Free-spacing mode: x

Allows for whitespace and comments within a regular expression. The whitespace and comments (starting with # and extending to the end of the line) are ignored by the regular expression engine.

Mode modifiers: (?i), (?-i), (?mod:...)

Usually, mode modifiers may be set within a regular expression with (?mod) to turn modes on for the rest of the current subexpression; (?-mod) to turn modes off for the rest of the current subexpression; and (?mod:...) to turn modes on or off between the colon and the closing parentheses. For example, use (?i:perl) matches use perl, use Perl, use PeRl, etc.

Comments: (?#...) *and* #

In free-spacing mode, # indicates that the rest of the line is a comment. When supported, the comment span (?#...) can be embedded anywhere in a regular expression, regardless of mode. For example, .{0,80}(?#Field limit is 80 chars) allows you to make notes about why you wrote .{0,80}.

Literal-text span: \Q...\E

Escapes metacharacters between \Q and \E. For example, \Q(.*)\E is the same as \(\.*\).

Grouping, capturing, conditionals, and control

This section covers syntax for grouping subpatterns, capturing submatches, conditional submatches, and quantifying the number of times a subpattern matches. (See MRE 137–142.)

Capturing and grouping parentheses: (...) *and* \1, \2, *etc.*

Parentheses perform two functions: grouping and capturing. Text matched by the subpattern within parentheses is captured for later use. Capturing parentheses are numbered by counting their opening parentheses from the left. If backreferences are available, the submatch can be referred to later in the same match with \1, \2, etc. The captured text is made available after a match by implementation-specific methods. For example, \b(\w+)\b \s+\1\b matches duplicate words, such as the the.

Grouping-only parentheses: (?:...)
Groups a subexpression, possibly for alternation or quantifiers, but does not capture the submatch. This is useful for efficiency and reusability. For example, (?:foobar) matches foobar, but does not save the match to a capture group.

Named capture: (?<name>...)
Performs capturing and grouping, with captured text later referenced by *name*. For example, Subject:(?<subject>.*) captures the text following Subject: to a capture group that can be referenced by the name subject.

Atomic grouping: (?>...)
Text matched within the group is never backtracked into, even if this leads to a match failure. For example, (?>[ab]*)\w\w matches aabbcc, but not aabbaa.

Alternation: ...|...
Allows several subexpressions to be tested. Alternation's low precedence sometimes causes subexpressions to be longer than intended, so use parentheses to specifically group what you want alternated. Thus, \b(foo|bar)\b matches the words foo or bar.

Conditional: (?(*if*)*then*|*else*)
The *if* is implementation-dependent, but generally is a reference to a captured subexpression or a lookaround. The *then* and *else* parts are both regular expression patterns. If the *if* part is true, the *then* is applied. Otherwise, *else* is applied. For example, (<)?foo(?(1)>|bar) matches <foo> as well as foobar.

Greedy quantifiers: *, +, ?, {*num,num* }
The greedy quantifiers determine how many times a construct may be applied. They attempt to match as many times as possible, but will backtrack and give up matches if necessary for the success of the overall match. For example, (ab)+ matches all of abababab.

Lazy quantifiers: *?, +?, ??, {*num,num* }?

Lazy quantifiers control how many times a construct may be applied. However, unlike greedy quantifiers, they attempt to match as few times as possible. For example, (an)+? matches only an of banana.

Possessive quantifiers: *+, ++, ?+, {*num,num* }+

Possessive quantifiers are like greedy quantifiers, except that they "lock in" their match, disallowing later backtracking to break up the submatch. For example, (ab)++ab will not match abababab.

Unicode Support

The *Unicode* character set gives unique numbers to the characters in all the world's languages. Because of the large number of possible characters, Unicode requires more than one byte to represent a character. Some regular expression implementations will not understand Unicode characters because they expect 1 byte ASCII characters. Basic support for Unicode characters starts with the ability to match a literal string of Unicode characters. Advanced support includes character classes and other constructs that incorporate characters from all Unicode-supported languages. For example, \w might match è; as well as e.

Regular Expression Cookbook

This section contains simple versions of common regular expression patterns. You may need to adjust them to meet your needs.

Each expression is presented here with target strings that it matches, and target strings that it does not match, so you can get a sense of what adjustments you may need to make for your own use cases.

They are written in the Perl style:

```
/pattern/mode
s/pattern/replacement/mode
```

Recipes

Removing leading and trailing whitespace

```
s/^\s+//
s/\s+$//
```

Matches: " foo bar ", "foo "

Nonmatches: "foo bar"

Numbers from 0 to 999999

```
/^\d{1,6}$/
```

Matches: 42, 678234

Nonmatches: 10,000

Valid HTML Hex code

```
/^#([a-fA-F0-9]){3}(([a-fA-F0-9]){3})?$/
```

Matches: #fff, #1a1, #996633

Nonmatches: #ff, FFFFFF

U.S. Social Security number

```
/^\d{3}-\d{2}-\d{4}$/
```

Matches: 078-05-1120

Nonmatches: 078051120, 1234-12-12

U.S. zip code

```
/^\d{5}(-\d{4})?$/
```

Matches: 94941-3232, 10024

Nonmatches: 949413232

U.S. currency

```
/^\$(\d{1,3}(\,\d{3})*|\d+)(\.\d{2})?$/
```

Matches: $20, $15,000.01

Nonmatches: $1.001, $.99

Match date: MM/DD/YYYY HH:MM:SS

```
/^\d\d/\d\d/\d\d\d\d \d\d:\d\d:\d\d$/
```

Matches: 04/30/1978 20:45:38

Nonmatches: 4/30/1978 20:45:38, 4/30/78

Leading pathname

```
/^.*\//
```

Matches: /usr/local/bin/apachectl

Nonmatches: C:\\System\foo.exe

(See MRE 190–192.)

Dotted Quad IP address

```
/^(\d|[01]?\d\d|2[0-4]\d|25[0-5])\.(\d|[01]?\d\d|2[0-4]
\d|25[0-5])\.
(\d|[01]?\d\d|2[0-4]\d|25[0-5])\.(\d|[01]?\d\d|2[0-4]
\d|25[0-5])$/
```

Matches: 127.0.0.1, 224.22.5.110

Nonmatches: 127.1

(See MRE 187–189.)

MAC address

```
/^([0-9a-fA-F]{2}:){5}[0-9a-fA-F]{2}$/
```

Matches: 01:23:45:67:89:ab

Nonmatches: 01:23:45, 0123456789ab

Email

```
/^[0-9a-zA-Z]([-.\w]*[0-9a-zA-Z_+])*@([0-9a-zA-Z][-\w]*
[0-9a-zA-Z]\.)+[a-zA-Z]{2,9}$/
```

Matches: *tony@example.com*, *tony@i-e.com*, tony@mail.
example.museum

Nonmatches: .@example.com, *tony@i-.com*, *tony@example.a*

(See MRE 70.)

HTTP URL

```
/(https?):\/\/([0-9a-zA-Z][-\w]*[0-9a-zA-Z]\.)+
[a-zA-Z]{2,9})
(:\d{1,4})?([-\w\/#~:.?+=&%@~]*)/
```

Matches: *https://example.com*, `http://foo.com:8080/bar.html`

Nonmatches: *ftp://foo.com*, *ftp://foo.com/*

Perl 5.8

Perl provides a rich set of regular-expression operators, constructs, and features, with more being added in each new release. Perl uses a Traditional NFA match engine. For an explanation of the rules behind an NFA engine, see "Introduction to Regexes and Pattern Matching."

This reference covers Perl version 5.8. A number of new features will be introduced in Perl 5.10; these are covered in Table 8. Unicode features were introduced in 5.6, but did not stabilize until 5.8. Most other features work in versions 5.004 and later.

Supported Metacharacters

Perl supports the metacharacters and metasequences listed in Table 3 through Table 7. To learn more about expanded definitions of each metacharacter, see "Regex Metacharacters, Modes, and Constructs."

Table 3. Perl character representations

Sequence	Meaning
\a	Alert (bell).
\b	Backspace; supported only in character class (outside of character class matches a word boundary).
\e	Esc character, x1B.
\n	Newline; x0A on Unix and Windows, x0D on Mac OS 9.
\r	Carriage return; x0D on Unix and Windows, x0A on Mac OS 9.

Table 3. Perl character representations (continued)

Sequence	Meaning
\f	Form feed, x0C.
\t	Horizontal tab, x09.
octal	Character specified by a two- or three-digit octal code.
\x*hex*	Character specified by a one- or two-digit hexadecimal code.
\x{*hex*}	Character specified by any hexadecimal code.
\c*char*	Named control character.
\N{*name*}	A named character specified in the Unicode standard or listed in PATH_TO_PERLLIB/unicode/Names.txt; requires use charnames ':full'.

Table 4. Perl character classes and class-like constructs

Class	Meaning
[...]	A single character listed, or contained in a listed range.
[^...]	A single character not listed, and not contained within a listed range.
[:*class*:]	POSIX-style character class valid only within a regex character class.
.	Any character except newline (unless single-line mode, /s).
\C	One byte; however, this may corrupt a Unicode character stream.
\X	Base character, followed by any number of Unicode combining characters.
\w	Word character, \p{IsWord}.
\W	Nonword character, \P{IsWord}.
\d	Digit character, \p{IsDigit}.
\D	Nondigit character, \P{IsDigit}.
\s	Whitespace character, \p{IsSpace}.
\S	Nonwhitespace character, \P{IsSpace}.
\p{*prop*}	Character contained by given Unicode property, script, or block.
\P{*prop*}	Character not contained by given Unicode property, script, or block.

Table 5. Perl anchors and zero-width tests

Sequence	Meaning
^	Start of string, or, in multiline match mode (/m), the position after any newline.
\A	Start of search string, in all match modes.
$	End of search string or the point before a string-ending newline, or, in multiline match mode (/m), the position before any newline.
\Z	End of string, or the point before a string-ending newline, in any match mode.
\z	End of string, in any match mode.
\G	Beginning of current search.
\b	Word boundary.
\B	Not-word-boundary.
(?=...)	Positive lookahead.
(?!...)	Negative lookahead.
(?<=...)	Positive lookbehind; fixed-length only.
(?<!...)	Negative lookbehind; fixed-length only.

Table 6. Perl comments and mode modifiers

Modifier	Meaning
/i	Case-insensitive matching.
/m	^ and $ match next to embedded \n.
/s	Dot (.) matches newline.
/x	Ignore whitespace, and allow comments (#) in pattern.
/o	Compile pattern only once.
(?mode)	Turn listed modes (one or more of xsmi) on for the rest of the subexpression.
(?-mode)	Turn listed modes (one or more of xsmi) off for the rest of the subexpression.
(?mode:...)	Turn listed modes (one or more of xsmi) on within parentheses.
(?-mode:...)	Turn listed modes (one or more of xsmi) off within parentheses.

Table 6. Perl comments and mode modifiers (continued)

Modifier	Meaning
(?#...)	Treat substring as a comment.
#...	Treat rest of line as a comment in /x mode.
\u	Force next character to uppercase.
\l	Force next character to lowercase.
\U	Force all following characters to uppercase.
\L	Force all following characters to lowercase.
\Q	Quote all following regex metacharacters.
\E	End a span started with \U, \L, or \Q.

Table 7. Perl grouping, capturing, conditional, and control

Sequence	Meaning
(...)	Group subpattern and capture submatch into \1,\2,...and $1, $2,....
\n	Contains text matched by the *n*th capture group.
(?:...)	Groups subpattern, but does not capture submatch.
(?>...)	Atomic grouping.
...|...	Try subpatterns in alternation.
*	Match 0 or more times.
+	Match 1 or more times.
?	Match 1 or 0 times.
{n}	Match exactly *n* times.
{n,}	Match at least *n* times.
{x,y}	Match at least *x* times, but no more than *y* times.
*?	Match 0 or more times, but as few times as possible.
+?	Match 1 or more times, but as few times as possible.
??	Match 0 or 1 times, but as few times as possible.
{n,}?	Match at least *n* times, but as few times as possible.
{x,y}?	Match at least *x* times, and no more than *y* times, but as few times as possible.

Table 7. Perl grouping, capturing, conditional, and control (continued)

Sequence	Meaning
(?(COND)...|...)	Match with if-then-else pattern, where *COND* is an integer referring to a backreference, or a lookaround assertion.
(?(COND)...)	Match with if-then pattern.
(?{CODE})	Execute embedded Perl code.
(??{CODE})	Match regex from embedded Perl code.

Table 8. New features in Perl 5.10

Modifier	Meaning
(?<name>...) or (?'name'...)	Named capture group.
\k<name> or \k'name'	Backreference to named capture group.
%+	Hash reference to the leftmost capture of a given name, $+{foo}.
%-	Hash reference to an array of all captures of a given name, $-{foo}[0].
\g{n} or \gn	Back reference to the *n*th capture.
\g{-n} or \g-n	Relative backreference to the *n*th previous capture.
(?n)	Recurse into the *n*th capture buffer.
(?&NAME)	Recurse into the named capture buffer.
(?R)	Recursively call the entire expression.
(?(DEFINE)...)	Define a subexpression that can be recursed into.
(*FAIL)	Fail submatch, and force the engine to backtrack.
(*ACCEPT)	Force engine to accept the match, even if there is more pattern to check.
(*PRUNE)	Cause the match to fail from the current starting position.
(*MARK:name)	Marks and names the current position in the string. The position is available in $REGMARK.
(*SKIP:name)	Reject all matches up to the point where the named *MARK* was executed.
(*THEN)	When backtracked into, skip to the next alternation.

Table 8. New features in Perl 5.10 (continued)

Modifier	Meaning
(*COMMIT)	When backtracked into, cause the match to fail outright.
/p	Mode modifier that enables the ${^PREMATCH}, ${MATCH}, and ${^POSTMATCH} variables.
\K	Exclude previously matched text from the final match.

Regular Expression Operators

Perl provides the built-in regular expression operators qr//, m//, and s///, as well as the split function. Each operator accepts a regular expression pattern string that is run through string and variable interpolation, and then compiled.

Regular expressions are often delimited with the forward slash, but you can pick any nonalphanumeric, non-whitespace character. Here are some examples:

```
qr#...#      m!...!      m{...}
s|...|...|   s[...][...] s<...>/.../
```

A match delimited by slashes (/.../) doesn't require a leading m:

```
/.../      #same as m/.../
```

Using the single quote as a delimiter suppresses interpolation of variables and the constructs \N{*name*}, \u, \l, \U, \L, \Q, and \E. Normally, these are interpolated before being passed to the regular expression engine.

qr// (Quote Regex)

qr/*PATTERN*/ismxo

Quote and compile *PATTERN* as a regular expression. The returned value may be used in a later pattern match or substitution. This saves time if the regular expression is going to be interpolated repeatedly. The match modes (or lack of), /ismxo, are locked in.

m// (Matching)

m/*PATTERN*/imsxocg

Match *PATTERN* against input string. In list context, returns a list of substrings matched by capturing parentheses, or else (1) for a successful match or () for a failed match. In scalar context, returns 1 for success, or "" for failure. /imsxo are optional mode modifiers. /cg are optional match modifiers. /g in scalar context causes the match to start from the end of the previous match. In list context, a /g match returns all matches, or all captured substrings from all matches. A failed /g match will reset the match start to the beginning of the string, unless the match is in combined /cg mode.

s/// (Substitution)

s/*PATTERN*/*REPLACEMENT*/egimosx

Match *PATTERN* in the input string, and replace the match text with *REPLACEMENT*, returning the number of successes. /imosx are optional mode modifiers. /g substitutes all occurrences of *PATTERN*. Each /e causes an evaluation of *REPLACEMENT* as Perl code.

split

split /*PATTERN*/, *EXPR*, *LIMIT*
split /*PATTERN*/, *EXPR*
split /*PATTERN*/
split

Return a list of substrings surrounding matches of *PATTERN* in *EXPR*. If *LIMIT* is included, the list contains substrings surrounding the first *LIMIT* matches. The pattern argument is a match operator, so use m if you want alternate delimiters (e.g., split m{*PATTERN*}). The match permits the same modifiers as m{}. Table 9 lists the after-match variables.

Table 9. Perl after-match variables

Variable	Meaning
$1, $2, ...	Captured submatches.
@-	$-[0]: offset of start of match. $-[n]: offset of start of $n.
@+	$+[0]: offset of end of match. $+[n]: offset of end of $n.
$+	Last parenthesized match.
$'	Text before match. Causes all regular expressions to be slower. Same as substr($input, 0, $-[0]).
$&	Text of match. Causes all regular expressions to be slower. Same as substr($input, $-[0], $+[0] - $-[0]).
$`	Text after match. Causes all regular expressions to be slower. Same as substr($input, $+[0]).
$^N	Text of most recently closed capturing parentheses.
$*	If true, /m is assumed for all matches without a /s.
$^R	The result value of the most recently executed code construct within a pattern match.

Unicode Support

Perl provides built-in support for Unicode 3.2, including full support in the \w, \d, \s, and \b metasequences.

The following constructs respect the current locale if use locale is defined: case-insensitive (i) mode, \L, \l, \U, \u, \w, and \W.

Perl supports the standard Unicode properties (see Table 3) as well as Perl-specific composite properties (see Table 10). Scripts and properties may have an Is prefix, but do not require it. Blocks require an In prefix only if the block name conflicts with a script name.

Table 10. Perl composite Unicode properties

Property	Equivalent
IsASCII	[\x00-\x7f]
IsAlnum	[\p{Ll}\p{Lu}\p{Lt}\p{Lo}\p{Nd}]
IsAlpha	[\p{Ll}\p{Lu}\p{Lt}\p{Lo}]
IsCntrl	\p{C}
IsDigit	\p{Nd}
IsGraph	[^\p{C}\p{Space}]
IsLower	\p{Ll}
IsPrint	\P{C}
IsPunct	\p{P}
IsSpace	[\t\n\f\r\p{Z}]
IsUppper	[\p{Lu}\p{Lt}]
IsWord	[_\p{Ll}\p{Lu}\p{Lt}\p{Lo}\p{Nd}]
IsXDigit	[0-9a-fA-F]

Examples

Example 1. Simple match

```
# Find Spider-Man, Spiderman, SPIDER-MAN, etc.
my $dailybugle = "Spider-Man Menaces City!";
if ($dailybugle =~ m/spider[- ]?man/i) { do_something(); }
```

Example 2. Match, capture group, and qr

```
# Match dates formatted like MM/DD/YYYY, MM-DD-YY,...
my $date  = "12/30/1969";
my $regex = qr!^(\d\d)[-/](\d\d)[-/](\d\d(?:\d\d)?)$!;
if ($date =~ $regex) {
  print "Day= ", $1,
        " Month=", $2,
        " Year= ", $3;
}
```

Example 3. Simple substitution

```perl
# Convert <br> to <br /> for XHTML compliance
my $text = "Hello World! <br>";
$text =~ s#<br>#<br />#ig;
```

Example 4. Harder substitution

```perl
# urlify - turn URLs into HTML links
$text = "Check the web site, http://www.oreilly.com/catalog/
regexppr.";
$text =~
    s{
      \b                             # start at word boundary
      (                              # capture to $1
       (https?|telnet|gopher|file|wais|ftp) :
                                     # resource and colon
       [\w/#~:.?+=&%@!\-] +?         # one or more valid
                                     # characters
                                     # but take as little as
                                     # possible
      )
      (?=                            # lookahead
        [.:?\-] *                    #  for possible punctuation
        (?: [^\w/#~:.?+=&%@!\-]      #  invalid character
          | $ )                      #  or end of string
      )
     }{<a href="$1">$1</a>}igox;
```

Other Resources

- *Programming Perl*, by Larry Wall et al. (O'Reilly), is the standard Perl reference.

- *Mastering Regular Expressions*, Third Edition, by Jeffrey E. F. Friedl (O'Reilly), covers the details of Perl regular expressions on pages 283–364.

- perlre is the perldoc documentation provided with most Perl distributions.

Java (java.util.regex)

Java 1.4 introduced regular expressions with Sun's java.util.regex package. Although there are competing packages available for previous versions of Java, Sun's is now the standard. Sun's package uses a Traditional NFA match engine. For an explanation of the rules behind a Traditional NFA engine, see "Introduction to Regexes and Pattern Matching." This section covers regular expressions in Java 1.5 and 1.6.

Supported Metacharacters

java.util.regex supports the metacharacters and metasequences listed in Table 11 through Table 15. For expanded definitions of each metacharacter, see "Regex Metacharacters, Modes, and Constructs."

Table 11. Java character representations

Sequence	Meaning
\a	Alert (bell).
\b	Backspace, \x08, supported only in character class.
\e	Esc character, \x1B.
\n	Newline, \x0A.
\r	Carriage return, \x0D.
\f	Form feed, \x0C.
\t	Horizontal tab, \x09.
\0*octal*	Character specified by a one-, two-, or three-digit octal code.
\x*hex*	Character specified by a two-digit hexadecimal code.
\u*hex*	Unicode character specified by a four-digit hexadecimal code.
\c*char*	Named control character.

Table 12. Java character classes and class-like constructs

Class	Meaning
[...]	A single character listed or contained in a listed range.
[^...]	A single character not liste and not contained within a listed range.
.	Any character, except a line terminator (unless DOTALL mode).
\w	Word character, [a-zA-Z0-9_].
\W	Nonword character, [^a-zA-Z0-9_].
\d	Digit, [0-9].
\D	Nondigit, [^0-9].
\s	Whitespace character, [\t\n\f\r\x0B].
\S	Nonwhitespace character, [^ \t\n\f\r\x0B].
\p{*prop*}	Character contained by given POSIX character class, Unicode property, or Unicode block.
\P{*prop*}	Character not contained by given POSIX character class, Unicode property, or Unicode block.

Table 13. Java anchors and other zero-width tests

Sequence	Meaning
^	Start of string, or the point after any newline if in MULTILINE mode.
\A	Beginning of string, in any match mode.
$	End of string, or the point before any newline if in MULTILINE mode.
\Z	End of string, but before any final line terminator, in any match mode.
\z	End of string, in any match mode.
\b	Word boundary.
\B	Not-word-boundary.
\G	Beginning of current search.

Table 13. Java anchors and other zero-width tests (continued)

Sequence	Meaning
(?=...)	Positive lookahead.
(?!...)	Negative lookahead.
(?<=...)	Positive lookbehind.
(?<!...)	Negative lookbehind.

Table 14. Java comments and mode modifiers

Modifier/sequence	Mode character	Meaning
Pattern.UNIX_LINES	d	Treat \n as the only line terminator.
Pattern.DOTALL	s	Dot (.) matches any character, including a line terminator.
Pattern.MULTILINE	m	^ and $ match next to embedded line terminators.
Pattern.COMMENTS	x	Ignore whitespace, and allow embedded comments starting with #.
Pattern.CASE_INSENSITIVE	i	Case-insensitive match for ASCII characters.
Pattern.UNICODE_CASE	u	Case-insensitive match for Unicode characters.
Pattern.CANON_EQ		Unicode "canonical equivalence" mode, where characters, or sequences of a base character and combining characters with identical visual representations, are treated as equals.
(?mode)		Turn listed modes (one or more of idmsux) on for the rest of the subexpression.
(?-mode)		Turn listed modes (one or more of idmsux) off for the rest of the subexpression.
(?mode:...)		Turn listed modes (one or more of idmsux) on within parentheses.

Table 14. Java comments and mode modifiers (continued)

Modifier/sequence	Mode character	Meaning
(?-mode:...)		Turn listed modes (one or more of idmsux) off within parentheses.
#...		Treat rest of line as a comment in /x mode.

Table 15. Java grouping, capturing, conditional, and control

Sequence	Meaning
(...)	Group subpattern and capture submatch into \1,\2,... and $1, $2,....
\n	Contains text matched by the nth capture group.
$n	In a replacement string, contains text matched by the nth capture group.
(?:...)	Groups subpattern, but does not capture submatch.
(?>...)	Atomic grouping.
...|...	Try subpatterns in alternation.
*	Match 0 or more times.
+	Match 1 or more times.
?	Match 1 or 0 times.
{n}	Match exactly n times.
{n,}	Match at least n times.
{x,y}	Match at least x times, but no more than y times.
*?	Match 0 or more times, but as few times as possible.
+?	Match 1 or more times, but as few times as possible.
??	Match 0 or 1 times, but as few times as possible.
{n,}?	Match at least n times, but as few times as possible.
{x,y}?	Match at least x times, no more than y times, and as few times as possible.
*+	Match 0 or more times, and never backtrack.
++	Match 1 or more times, and never backtrack.

Table 15. Java grouping, capturing, conditional, and control (continued)

Sequence	Meaning
?+	Match 0 or 1 times, and never backtrack.
{*n*}+	Match at least *n* times, and never backtrack.
{*n*,}+	Match at least *n* times, and never backtrack.
{*x,y*}+	Match at least *x* times, no more than *y* times, and never backtrack.

Regular Expression Classes and Interfaces

Regular expression functions are contained in two main classes, java.util.regex.Pattern and java.util.regex.Matcher; an exception, java.util.regex.PatternSyntaxException; and an interface, CharSequence. Additionally, the String class implements the CharSequence interface to provide basic pattern-matching methods. Pattern objects are compiled regular expressions that can be applied to any CharSequence. A Matcher is a stateful object that scans for one or more occurrences of a Pattern applied in a string (or any object implementing CharSequence).

Backslashes in regular expression String literals need to be escaped. So, \n (newline) becomes \\n when used in a Java String literal that is to be used as a regular expression.

java.lang.String

Description

Methods for pattern matching.

Methods

boolean matches(String *regex*)
    Return true if *regex* matches the entire String.

String[ ] split(String *regex*)
    Return an array of the substrings surrounding matches of *regex*.

```
String [ ] split(String regex, int limit)
```
Return an array of the substrings surrounding the first *limit*-1 matches of *regex*.

```
String replaceFirst(String regex, String replacement)
```
Replace the substring matched by *regex* with *replacement*.

```
String replaceAll(String regex, String replacement)
```
Replace all substrings matched by *regex* with *replacement*.

java.util.regex.Pattern

Description

Models a regular expression pattern.

Methods

```
static Pattern compile(String regex)
```
Construct a Pattern object from *regex*.

```
static Pattern compile(String regex, int flags)
```
Construct a new Pattern object out of *regex*, and the OR'd mode-modifier constants *flags*.

```
int flags( )
```
Return the Pattern's mode modifiers.

```
Matcher matcher(CharSequence input)
```
Construct a Matcher object that will match this Pattern against *input*.

```
static boolean matches(String regex, CharSequence input)
```
Return true if *regex* matches the entire string *input*.

```
String pattern( )
```
Return the regular expression used to create this Pattern.

```
static String quote(String text)
```
Escapes the text so that regular expression operators will be matched literally.

```
String[ ] split(CharSequence input)
```
Return an array of the substrings surrounding matches of this Pattern in *input*.

```
String[ ] split(CharSequence input, int limit)
```
Return an array of the substrings surrounding the first *limit* matches of this pattern in *regex*.

java.util.regex.Matcher

Description

Models a stateful regular expression pattern matcher and pattern matching results.

Methods

Matcher appendReplacement(StringBuffer *sb*, String *replacement*)
    Append substring preceding match and *replacement* to *sb*.

StringBuffer appendTail(StringBuffer *sb*)
    Append substring following end of match to *sb*.

int end( )
    Index of the first character after the end of the match.

int end(int *group*)
    Index of the first character after the text captured by *group*.

boolean find( )
    Find the next match in the input string.

boolean find(int *start*)
    Find the next match after character position *start*.

String group( )
    Text matched by this Pattern.

String group(int *group*)
    Text captured by capture group *group*.

int groupCount( )
    Number of capturing groups in Pattern.

boolean hasAnchoringBounds( )
    Return true if this Matcher uses anchoring bounds so that anchor operators match at the region boundaries, not just at the start and end of the target string.

boolean hasTransparentBounds( )
    True if this Matcher uses transparent bounds so that lookaround operators can see outside the current search bounds. Defaults to false.

boolean hitEnd( )
    True if the last match attempts to inspect beyond the end of the input. In scanners, this is an indication that more input may have resulted in a longer match.

`boolean lookingAt( )`
> True if the pattern matches at the beginning of the input.

`boolean matches( )`
> Return true if Pattern matches entire input string.

`Pattern pattern( )`
> Return Pattern object used by this Matcher.

`static String quoteReplacement(String string)`
> Escape special characters evaluated during replacements.

`Matcher region(int start, int end)`
> Return this matcher and run future matches in the region between start characters and end characters from the beginning of the string.

`int regionStart( )`
> Return the starting offset of the search region. Defaults to zero.

`int regionEnd( )`
> Return the ending offset of the search region. Defaults to the length of the target string.

`String replaceAll(String replacement)`
> Replace every match with replacement.

`String replaceFirst(String replacement)`
> Replace first match with replacement.

`boolean requireEnd( )`
> Return true if the success of the last match relied on the end of the input. In scanners, this is an indication that more input may have caused a failed match.

`Matcher reset( )`
> Reset this matcher so that the next match starts at the beginning of the input string.

`Matcher reset(CharSequence input)`
> Reset this matcher with new input.

`int start( )`
> Index of first character matched.

`int start(int group)`
> Index of first character matched in captured substring group.

`MatchResult toMatchResult( )`
> Return a MatchResult object for the most recent match.

`String toString( )`
> Return a string representation of the matcher for debugging.

`Matcher useAnchorBounds(boolean b)`

If true, set the `Matcher` to use anchor bounds so that anchor operators match at the beginning and end of the current search bounds, rather than the beginning and end of the search string. Defaults to true.

`Matcher usePattern(Pattern p)`

Replace the `Matcher`'s pattern, but keep the rest of the match state.

`Matcher useTransparentBounds(boolean b)`

If true, set the `Matcher` to use transparent bounds so that lookaround operators can see outside of the current search bounds. Defaults to false.

java.util.regex.PatternSyntaxException

Description

Thrown to indicate a syntax error in a regular expression pattern.

Methods

`PatternSyntaxException(String desc, String regex, int index)`

Construct an instance of this class.

`String getDescription( )`

Return error description.

`int getIndex( )`

Return error index.

`String getMessage( )`

Return a multiline error message containing error description, index, regular expression pattern, and indication of the position of the error within the pattern.

`String getPattern( )`

Return the regular expression pattern that threw the exception.

java.lang.CharSequence

Description

Defines an interface for read-only access so that regular expression patterns may be applied to a sequence of characters.

Methods

```
char charAt(int index)
```
> Return the character at the zero-based position *index*.

```
int length( )
```
> Return the number of characters in the sequence.

```
CharSequence subSequence(int start, int end)
```
> Return a subsequence, including the *start* index, and excluding the *end* index.

```
String toString( )
```
> Return a String representation of the sequence.

Unicode Support

This package supports Unicode 4.0, although \w, \W, \d, \D, \s, and \S support only ASCII. You can use the equivalent Unicode properties \p{L}, \P{L}, \p{Nd}, \P{Nd}, \p{Z}, and \P{Z}. The word boundary sequences—\b and \B—do understand Unicode.

For supported Unicode properties and blocks, see Table 2. This package supports only the short property names, such as \p{Lu}, and not \p{Lowercase_Letter}. Block names require the In prefix, and support only the name form without spaces or underscores, for example, \p{InGreekExtended}, not \p{In_Greek_Extended} or \p{In Greek Extended}.

Examples

Example 5. Simple match

```
import java.util.regex.*;

// Find Spider-Man, Spiderman, SPIDER-MAN, etc.
public class StringRegexTest {
  public static void main(String[] args) throws Exception {
    String dailyBugle = "Spider-Man Menaces City!";

    //regex must match entire string
```

Example 5. Simple match (continued)

```java
    String regex = "(?i).*spider[- ]?man.*";

    if (dailyBugle.matches(regex)) {
      System.out.println("Matched: " + dailyBugle);
    }
  }
}
```

Example 6. Match and capture group

```java
// Match dates formatted like MM/DD/YYYY, MM-DD-YY,...
import java.util.regex.*;

public class MatchTest {
  public static void main(String[] args) throws Exception {
    String date = "12/30/1969";
    Pattern p =
      Pattern.compile("^(\\d\\d)[-/](\\d\\d)[-/](\\d\\d(?:\\d\\d)?)$");

    Matcher m = p.matcher(date);

    if (m.find()) {
      String month = m.group(1);
      String day   = m.group(2);
      String year  = m.group(3);
      System.out.printf("Found %s-%s-%s\n", year, month, day);
    }
  }
}
```

Example 7. Simple substitution

```java
// Example -. Simple substitution
// Convert <br> to <br /> for XHTML compliance
import java.util.regex.*;

public class SimpleSubstitutionTest {
  public static void main(String[] args) {
    String text = "Hello world. <br>";
```

Example 7. Simple substitution (continued)

```
    Pattern p = Pattern.compile("<br>", Pattern.CASE_
INSENSITIVE);
    Matcher m = p.matcher(text);

    String result = m.replaceAll("<br />");
    System.out.println(result);
  }
}
```

Example 8. Harder substitution

```
// urlify - turn URLs into HTML links
import java.util.regex.*;

public class Urlify {
  public static void main (String[ ] args) throws Exception {
    String text = "Check the web site, http://www.oreilly.com/
catalog/regexppr.";
    String regex =
        "\\b                        # start at word\n"
    +  "                            # boundary\n"
    +  "(                           # capture to $1\n"
    +  "(https?|telnet|gopher|file|wais|ftp) : \n"
    +  "                            # resource and colon\n"
    +  "[\\w/\\#~:.?+=&%@!\\-] +?    # one or more valid\n"
    +  "                            # characters\n"
    +  "                            # but take as little\n"
    +  "                            # as possible\n"
    +  ")\n"
    +  "(?=                         # lookahead\n"
    +  "[.:?\\-] *                  # for possible punc\n"
    +  "(?: [^\\w/\\#~:.?+=&%@!\\-] # invalid character\n"
    +  "| $ )                       # or end of string\n"
    +  ")";

    Pattern p = Pattern.compile(regex,
        Pattern.CASE_INSENSITIVE + Pattern.COMMENTS);
    Matcher m = p.matcher(text);
    String result = m.replaceAll("<a href=\"$1\">$1</a>");
    System.out.println(result);
  }
}
```

Other Resources

- *Mastering Regular Expressions*, Third Edition, by Jeffrey E. F. Friedl (O'Reilly), covers the details of Java regular expressions on pages 365–403.

- Sun's online documentation at *http://java.sun.com/javase/ 6/docs/api/java/util/regex/package-summary.html*.

.NET and C#

Microsoft's .NET Framework provides a consistent and powerful set of regular expression classes for all .NET implementations. The following sections list the .NET regular expression syntax, the core .NET classes, and C# examples. Microsoft's .NET uses a Traditional NFA match engine. For an explanation of the rules behind this engine, see "Introduction to Regexes and Pattern Matching."

Supported Metacharacters

.NET supports the metacharacters and metasequences listed in Table 16 through Table 21. For expanded definitions of each metacharacter, see "Regex Metacharacters, Modes, and Constructs."

Table 16. .NET character representations

Sequence	Meaning
\a	Alert (bell), \x07.
\b	Backspace, \x08, supported only in character class.
\e	Esc character, \x1B.
\n	Newline, \x0A.
\r	Carriage return, \x0D.
\f	Form feed, \x0C.

Table 16. .NET character representations (continued)

Sequence	Meaning
\t	Horizontal tab, \x09.
\v	Vertical tab, \x0B.
\0*octal*	Character specified by a two-digit octal code.
\x*hex*	Character specified by a two-digit hexadecimal code.
\u*hex*	Character specified by a four-digit hexadecimal code.
\c*char*	Named control character.

Table 17. .NET character classes and class-like constructs

Class	Meaning
[...]	A single character listed, or contained within a listed range.
[^...]	A single character not listed, and not contained within a listed range.
.	Any character, except a line terminator (unless single-line mode, s).
\w	Word character, [\p{Ll}\p{Lu}\p{Lt}\p{Lo}\p{Nd}\p{Pc}] or [a-zA-Z_0-9] in ECMAScript mode.
\W	Nonword character, [\p{Ll}\p{Lu}\p{Lt}\p{Lo}\p{Nd}\p{Pc}], or [^a-zA-Z_0-9] in ECMAScript mode.
\d	Digit, \p{Nd}, or [0-9] in ECMAScript mode.
\D	Nondigit, \P{Nd}, or [^0-9] in ECMAScript mode.
\s	Whitespace character, [\f\n\r\t\v\x85\p{Z}] or [\f\n\r\t\v] in ECMAScript mode.
\S	Nonwhitespace character, [^ \f\n\r\t\v\x85\p{Z}] or [^ \f\n\r\t\v] in ECMAScript mode.
\p{*prop*}	Character contained by given Unicode block or property.
\P{*prop*}	Character not contained by given Unicode block or property.

Table 18. .NET anchors and other zero-width tests

Sequence	Meaning
^	Start of string, or the point after any newline if in MULTILINE mode.
\A	Beginning of string, in all match modes.
$	End of string, or the point before any newline if in MULTILINE mode.
\Z	End of string, but before any final line terminator, in all match modes.
\z	End of string, in all match modes.
\b	Boundary between a \w character, and a \W character.
\B	Not-word-boundary.
\G	End of the previous match.
(?=...)	Positive lookahead.
(?!...)	Negative lookahead.
(?<=...)	Positive lookbehind.
(?<!...)	Negative lookbehind.

Table 19. .NET comments and mode modifiers

Modifier/sequence	Mode character	Meaning
Singleline	s	Dot (.) matches any character, including a line terminator.
Multiline	m	^ and $ match next to embedded line terminators.
IgnorePatternWhite space	x	Ignore whitespace, and allow embedded comments starting with #.
IgnoreCase	i	Case-insensitive match based on characters in the current culture.
CultureInvariant	i	Culture-insensitive match.
ExplicitCapture	n	Allow named capture groups, but treat parentheses as noncapturing groups.

Table 19. .NET comments and mode modifiers (continued)

Modifier/sequence	Mode character	Meaning
Compiled		Compile regular expression.
RightToLeft		Search from right to left, starting to the left of the start position. This has undefined and unpredictable semantics.
ECMAScript		Enables ECMAScript compliance when used with IgnoreCase or Multiline.
(?imnsx-imnsx)		Turn match flags on or off for rest of pattern.
(?imnsx-imnsx:...)		Turn match flags on or off for the rest of the subexpression.
(?#...)		Treat substring as a comment.
#...		Treat rest of line as a comment in /x mode.

Table 20. .NET grouping, capturing, conditional, and control

Sequence	Meaning
(...)	Grouping. Submatches fill \1,\2,... and $1, $2,....
\n	In a regular expression, match what was matched by the *n*th earlier submatch.
$n	In a replacement string, contains the *n*th earlier submatch.
(?<name>...)	Captures matched substring into group, *name*.
(?:...)	Grouping-only parentheses, no capturing.
(?>...)	Atomic grouping.
...|...	Alternation; match one or the other.
*	Match 0 or more times.
+	Match 1 or more times.
?	Match 1 or 0 times.

Table 20. .NET grouping, capturing, conditional,
and control (continued)

Sequence	Meaning
{n}	Match exactly n times.
{n,}	Match at least n times.
{x,y}	Match at least x times, but no more than y times.
*?	Match 0 or more times, but as few times as possible.
+?	Match 1 or more times, but as few times as possible.
??	Match 0 or 1 times, but as few times as possible.
{n,}?	Match at least n times, but as few times as possible.
{x,y}?	Match at least x times, and no more than y times, but as few times as possible.

Table 21. .NET replacement sequences

Sequence	Meaning
$1, $2, ...	Captured submatches.
${name}	Matched text of a named capture group.
$'	Text before match.
$&	Text of match.
$`	Text after match.
$+	Last parenthesized match.
$_	Copy of original input string.

Regular Expression Classes and Interfaces

.NET defines its regular expression support in the System.
Text.RegularExpressions module. The RegExp( ) constructor
handles regular expression creation, and the rest of the
RegExp methods handle pattern matching. The Groups and
Match classes contain information about each match.

C#'s raw string syntax, @"", allows defining regular expression patterns without having to escape embedded backslashes.

Regex

This class handles the creation of regular expressions and pattern matching. Several static methods allow for pattern matching without creating a RegExp object.

Methods

```
public Regex(string pattern)
```

```
public Regex(string pattern, RegexOptions options)
```
Return a regular expression object based on *pattern*, and with the optional mode modifiers, *options*.

```
public static void CompileToAssembly(RegexCompilationInfo[ ]
regexinfos, System.Reflection.AssemblyName assemblyname)
```

```
public static void CompileToAssembly(RegexCompilationInfo[ ]
regexinfos, System.Reflection.AssemblyName assemblyname)
```

```
public static void CompileToAssembly(RegexCompilationInfo[ ]
regexinfos,    System.Reflection.AssemblyName    assemblyname,
System.Reflection.Emit.CustomAttributeBuilder[ ] attributes)
```

```
public static void CompileToAssembly(RegexCompilationInfo[ ]
regexinfos,    System.Reflection.AssemblyName    assemblyname,
System.Reflection.Emit.CustomAttributeBuilder[ ] attributes,
string resourceFile)
```
Compile one or more Regex objects to an assembly. The *regexinfos* array describes the regular expressions to include. The assembly filename is *assemblyname*. The array *attributes* defines attributes for the assembly. *resourceFile* is the name of a Win32 resource file to include in the assembly.

```
public static string Escape(string str)
```
Return a string with all regular expression metacharacters, pound characters (#), and whitespace escaped.

```
public static bool IsMatch(string input, string pattern)
```

```
public static bool IsMatch(string input, string pattern,
RegexOptions options)
```

```
public bool IsMatch(string input)
```

```
public bool IsMatch(string input, int startat)
```

Return the success of a single match against the input string *input*. Static versions of this method require the regular expression *pattern*. The *options* parameter allows for optional mode modifiers (OR'd together). The *startat* parameter defines a starting position in *input* to start matching.

```
public static Match Match(string input, string pattern)
```

```
public static Match Match(string input, string pattern,
RegExpOptions options)
```

```
public Match Match(string input)
```

```
public Match Match(string input, int startat)
```

```
public Match Match(string input, int startat, int length)
```

Perform a single match against the input string *input*, and return information about the match in a Match object. Static versions of this method require the regular expression *pattern*. The *options* parameter allows for optional mode modifiers (OR'd together). The *startat* and *length* parameters define a starting position, and the number of characters after the starting position to perform the match, respectively.

```
public static MatchCollection Matches(string input, string
pattern)
```

```
public static MatchCollection Matches(string input, string
pattern, RegExpOptions options)
```

```
public MatchCollection Matches(string input)
```

```
public MatchCollection Matches(string input, int startat)
```

Find all matches in the input string *input*, and return information about the matches in a MatchCollection object. Static versions of this method require the regular expression *pattern*. The *options* parameter allows for optional mode modifiers (OR'd together). The *startat* parameter defines a starting position in *input* to perform the match.

```
public    static    string    Replace(string    input,    pattern,
MatchEvaluator evaluator)

public    static    string    Replace(string    input,    pattern,
MatchEvaluator evaluator, RegexOptions options)

public static string Replace(string input, pattern, string
replacement)

public static string Replace(string input, pattern, string
replacement, RegexOptions options)

public string Replace(string input, MatchEvaluator evaluator)

public string Replace(string input, MatchEvaluator evaluator,
int count)

public string Replace(string input, MatchEvaluator evaluator,
int count, int startat)

public string Replace(string input, string replacement)

public string Replace(string input, string replacement, int count)

public  string  Replace(string  input,  string  replacement,  int
count, int startat)
```

> Return a string in which each match in *input* is replaced with
> the evaluation of the *replacement* string, or a call to a
> MatchEvaluator object. The string *replacement* can contain
> backreferences to captured text with the $*n* or ${*name*} syntax.

> The *options* parameter allows for optional mode modifiers
> (OR'd together). The *count* parameter limits the number of
> replacements. The *startat* parameter defines a starting posi-
> tion in *input* to start the replacement.

```
public static string[ ] Split(string input, string pattern)

public static string[ ] Split(string input, string pattern,
RegexOptions options)

public static string[ ] Split(string input)

public static string[ ] Split(string input, int count)

public static string[ ] Split(string input, int count, int
startat)
```

> Return an array of strings broken around matches of the regex
> pattern. If specified, no more than *count* strings are returned.
> You can specify a starting position in *input* with *startat*.

Match

Properties

`public bool Success`
Indicate whether the match was successful.

`public string Value`
Text of the match.

`public int Length`
Number of characters in the matched text.

`public int Index`
Zero-based character index of the start of the match.

`public GroupCollection Groups`
A `GroupCollection` object, where `Groups[0].value` contains the text of the entire match, and each additional `Groups` element contains the text matched by a capture group.

Methods

`public Match NextMatch( )`
Return a `Match` object for the next match of the regex in the input string.

`public virtual string Result(string result)`
Return *result* with special replacement sequences replaced by values from the previous match.

`public static Match Synchronized(Match inner)`
Return a `Match` object identical to *inner*, except also safe for multithreaded use.

Group

Properties

`public bool Success`
True if the group participated in the match.

`public string Value`
Text captured by this group.

```
public int Length
    Number of characters captured by this group.
public int Index
    Zero-based character index of the start of the text captured by
    this group.
```

Unicode Support

.NET provides built-in support for Unicode 3.1, including full
support in the \w, \d, and \s sequences. The range of characters matched can be limited to ASCII characters by turning on
ECMAScript mode. Case-insensitive matching is limited to the
characters of the current language defined in Thread.
CurrentCulture, unless the CultureInvariant option is set.

.NET supports the standard Unicode properties (see Table 2)
and blocks. Only the short form of property names are supported. Block names require the Is prefix, and must use the
simple name form, without spaces or underscores.

Examples

Example 9. Simple match

```
//Find Spider-Man, Spiderman, SPIDER-MAN, etc.
namespace Regex_PocketRef
{
  using System.Text.RegularExpressions;

  class SimpleMatchTest
  {
    static void Main( )
    {
      string dailybugle = "Spider-Man Menaces City!";

      string regex = "spider[- ]?man";
```

Example 9. Simple match (continued)

```
    if (Regex.IsMatch(dailybugle, regex, RegexOptions.
IgnoreCase)) {
      //do something
    }
  }
}
```

Example 10. Match and capture group

```
//Match dates formatted like MM/DD/YYYY, MM-DD-YY,...
using System.Text.RegularExpressions;

class MatchTest
{
  static void Main()
  {
    string date = "12/30/1969";
    Regex r =
      new Regex( @"^(\d\d)[-/](\d\d)[-/](\d\d(?:\d\d)?)$" );

    Match m = r.Match(date);

    if (m.Success) {
      string month = m.Groups[1].Value;
      string day   = m.Groups[2].Value;
      string year  = m.Groups[3].Value;
    }
  }
}
```

Example 11. Simple substitution

```
//Convert <br> to <br /> for XHTML compliance
using System.Text.RegularExpressions;

class SimpleSubstitutionTest
{
  static void Main()
  {
    string text = "Hello world. <br>";
    string regex = "<br>";
```

Example 11. Simple substitution (continued)

```
    string replacement = "<br />";

    string result =
      Regex.Replace(text, regex, replacement, RegexOptions.
IgnoreCase);
  }
}
```

Example 12. Harder substitution

```
//urlify - turn URLs into HTML links
using System.Text.RegularExpressions;

public class Urlify
{
  static Main ()
  {
    string text = "Check the web site, http://www.oreilly.com/
catalog/regexppr.";
    string regex =
        @"\b                               # start at word boundary
          (                                # capture to $1
          (https?|telnet|gopher|file|wais|ftp) :
                                           # resource and colon
          [\w/#~:.?+=&%@!\-] +?             # one or more valid
                                           # characters
                                           # but take as little as
                                           # possible
        )
          (?=                              # lookahead
          [.:?\-] *                        # for possible
                                           # punctuation
          (?: [^\w/#~:.?+=&%@!\-]           # invalid character
          | $ )                            # or end of string
          )";

    Regex r = new Regex(regex, RegexOptions.IgnoreCase
                    | RegexOptions.IgnorePatternWhitespace);
    string result = r.Replace(text, "<a href=\"$1\">$1</a>");
  }
}
```

Other Resources

- *Programming C#*, by Jesse Liberty (O'Reilly), gives a thorough introduction to C#, .NET, and regular expressions.

- *Mastering Regular Expressions*, Third Edition, by Jeffrey E. F. Friedl (O'Reilly), covers the details of .NET regular expressions on pages 399–432.

- Microsoft's online documentation at *http://msdn.microsoft. com/library/default.asp?url=/library/en-us/cpgenref/html/ cpconregularexpressionslanguageelements.asp*.

PHP

This reference covers PHP 4.4.3 and 5.1.4's Perl-style regular expression support contained within the preg routines. Both are based on the PCRE 6.6 library. The preg routines use a Traditional NFA match engine. For an explanation of the rules behind an NFA engine, see "Introduction to Regexes and Pattern Matching."

Supported Metacharacters

PHP supports the metacharacters and metasequences listed in Table 22 through Table 26. For expanded definitions of each metacharacter, see "Regex Metacharacters, Modes, and Constructs."

Table 22. PHP character representations

Sequence	Meaning
\a	Alert (bell), \x07.
\b	Backspace, \x08, supported only in character class.
\e	Esc character, \x1B.
\n	Newline, \x0A.
\r	Carriage return, \x0D.
\f	Form feed, \x0C.

Table 22. PHP character representations (continued)

Sequence	Meaning
\t	Horizontal tab, \x09.
\octal	Character specified by a three-digit octal code.
\xhex	Character specified by a one- or two-digit hexadecimal code.
\x{hex}	Character specified by any hexadecimal code.
\cchar	Named control character.

Table 23. PHP character classes and class-like constructs

Class	Meaning
[...]	A single character listed or contained within a listed range.
[^...]	A single character not listed and not contained within a listed range.
[:class:]	POSIX-style character class (valid only within a regex character class).
.	Any character except newline (unless single-line mode, /s).
\C	One byte (this might corrupt a Unicode character stream, however).
\w	Word character, [a-zA-z0-9_].
\W	Nonword character, [^a-zA-z0-9_].
\d	Digit character, [0-9].
\D	Nondigit character, [^0-9].
\s	Whitespace character, [\n\r\f\t].
\S	Nonwhitespace character, [^\n\r\f\t].

Table 24. PHP anchors and zero-width tests

Sequence	Meaning
^	Start of string, or the point after any newline if in multiline match mode, /m.
\A	Start of search string, in all match modes.
$	End of search string, or the point before a string-ending newline, or before any newline if in multiline match mode, /m.

Table 24. PHP anchors and zero-width tests (continued)

Sequence	Meaning
\Z	End of string, or the point before a string-ending newline, in any match mode.
\z	End of string, in any match mode.
\G	Beginning of current search.
\b	Word boundary; position between a word character (\w), and a nonword character (\W), the start of the string, or the end of the string.
\B	Not-word-boundary.
(?=...)	Positive lookahead.
(?!...)	Negative lookahead.
(?<=...)	Positive lookbehind.
(?<!...)	Negative lookbehind.

Table 25. PHP comments and mode modifiers

Modes	Meaning
i	Case-insensitive matching.
m	^ and $ match next to embedded \n.
s	Dot (.) matches newline.
x	Ignore whitespace, and allow comments (#) in pattern.
U	Inverts greediness of all quantifiers: * becomes lazy, and *? greedy.
A	Force match to start at beginning of subject string.
D	Force $ to match end of string instead of before the string-ending newline. Overridden by multiline mode.
u	Treat regular expression and subject strings as strings of multibyte UTF-8 characters.
(?mode)	Turn listed modes (one or more of imsxU) on for the rest of the subexpression.
(?-mode)	Turn listed modes (one or more of imsxU) off for the rest of the subexpression.
(?mode:...)	Turn mode (xsmi) on within parentheses.
(?-mode:...)	Turn mode (xsmi) off within parentheses.

Table 25. PHP comments and mode modifiers (continued)

Modes	Meaning
(?#...)	Treat substring as a comment.
#...	Rest of line is treated as a comment in x mode.
\Q	Quotes all following regex metacharacters.
\E	Ends a span started with \Q.

Table 26. PHP grouping, capturing, conditional, and control

Sequence	Meaning
(...)	Group subpattern and capture submatch into \1, \2,....
(?P<name>...)	Group subpattern, and capture submatch into named capture group, *name*.
\n	Contains the results of the *n*th earlier submatch from a parentheses capture group, or a named capture group.
(?:...)	Groups subpattern, but does not capture submatch.
(?>...)	Atomic grouping.
...|...	Try subpatterns in alternation.
*	Match 0 or more times.
+	Match 1 or more times.
?	Match 1 or 0 times.
{n}	Match exactly *n* times.
{n,}	Match at least *n* times.
{x,y}	Match at least *x* times, but no more than *y* times.
*?	Match 0 or more times, but as few times as possible.
+?	Match 1 or more times, but as few times as possible.
??	Match 0 or 1 times, but as few times as possible.
{n,}?	Match at least *n* times, but as few times as possible.
{x,y}?	Match at least *x* times, no more than *y* times, and as few times as possible.
*+	Match 0 or more times, and never backtrack.
++	Match 1 or more times, and never backtrack.

Table 26. PHP grouping, capturing, conditional, and control (continued)

Sequence	Meaning
?+	Match 0 or 1 times, and never backtrack.
{*n*,}+	Match at least *n* times, and never backtrack.
{*x*,*y*}+	Match at least *x* times, no more than *y* times, and never backtrack.
(?(*condition*)...|...)	Match with if-then-else pattern. The *condition* can be the number of a capture group, or a lookahead or lookbehind construct.
(?(*condition*)...)	Match with if-then pattern. The *condition* can be the number of a capture group, or a lookahead or lookbehind construct.

Pattern-Matching Functions

PHP provides several standalone functions for pattern matching. When creating regular expression strings, you need to escape embedded backslashes; otherwise, the backslash is interpreted in the string before being sent to the regular expression engine.

array preg_grep (string *pattern*, array *input*)

Return array containing every element of *input* matched by *pattern*.

int preg_match_all (string *pattern*, string *subject*, array *matches* [, int *flags*])

Search for all matches of *pattern* against *subject*, and return the number of matches. The matched substrings are placed in the *matches* array. The first element of *matches* is an array containing the text of each full match. Each additional element *n* of *matches* is an array containing the *n*th capture group match for each full match. So, for example, matches[7][3] contains the text matches by the seventh capture group in the fourth match of *pattern* in *subject*.

The default ordering of *matches* can be set explicitly with the PREG_SET_ORDER flag. PREG_SET_ORDER sets a more intuitive ordering, where each element of *matches* is an array corresponding to a match. Element 0 of each array is the complete match, and each additional element corresponds to a capture group. The additional flag PREG_OFFSET_CAPTURE causes each array element containing a string to be replaced with a two-element array containing the same string and starting character position in *subject*.

int preg_match (string *pattern*, string *subject* [, array *matches* [, int *flags*]])

Return 1 if *pattern* matches in *subject*; otherwise, return 0. If the *matches* array is provided, the matched substring is placed in matches[0], and any capture group matches are placed in subsequent elements. One allowed flag, PREG_OFFSET_CAPTURE, causes elements of *matches* to be replaced with a two-element array containing the matched string and starting character position of the match.

string preg_quote (string *str* [, string *delimiter*])

Return a *str* with all regular expression metacharacters escaped. Provide the *delimiter* parameter if you are using optional delimiters with your regular expression, and need the delimiter escaped in *str*.

mixed preg_replace_callback (mixed *pattern*, callback *callback*, mixed *subject* [, int *limit*])

Return text of *subject* with every occurrence of *pattern* replaced with the results of *callback*. The callback should take one parameter, an array containing the matched text, and any matches from capture groups. If *limit* is provided, the function performs no more than *limit* replacements.

If *pattern* is an array, each element is replaced with *callback*. If *subject* is an array, the function iterates over each element.

```
mixed preg_replace (mixed pattern, mixed replacement, mixed
subject [, int limit])
```
Return text of *subject* with every occurrence of *pattern* replaced with *replacement*. If *limit* is provided, the function performs no more than *limit* replacements. The replacement string may refer to the match, or capture group matches with $n (preferred), or \n (deprecated). If *pattern* has the /e modifier, *replacement* is parsed for reference substitution, and then executed as PHP code.

If *pattern* is an array, each element is replaced with *replacement*, or, if *replacement* is an array, the corresponding element in *replacement*. If *subject* is an array, the function iterates over each element.

```
array preg_split (string pattern, string subject [, int
limit [, int flags]])
```
Return an array of strings broken around *pattern*. If *limit* is specified, preg_split( ) returns no more than *limit* substrings. A *limit* of –1 is the same as "no limit," allowing you to set flags. Available flags are: PREG_SPLIT_NO_EMPTY, return only nonempty pieces; PREG_SPLIT_DELIM_CAPTURE, return captured submatches after each split substring; and PREG_SPLIT_OFFSET_CAPTURE, return an array of two-element arrays where the first element is the match, and the second element is the offset of the match in *subject*.

Examples

Example 13. Simple match

```
//Find Spider-Man, Spiderman, SPIDER-MAN, etc.
$dailybugle = "Spider-Man Menaces City!";

$regex = "/spider[- ]?man/i";

if (preg_match($regex, $dailybugle)) {
     //do something
}
```

Example 14. Match and capture group

```
//Match dates formatted like MM/DD/YYYY, MM-DD-YY,...
$date = "12/30/1969";
$p    = "!^(\\d\\d)[-/](\\d\\d)[-/](\\d\\d(?:\\d\\d)?)$!";

if (preg_match($p,$date,$matches) {
     $month = $matches[1];
     $day   = $matches[2];
     $year  = $matches[3];
}
```

Example 15. Simple substitution

```
//Convert <br> to <br /> for XHTML compliance
$text = "Hello world. <br>";

$pattern = "{<br>}i";

echo preg_replace($pattern, "<br />", $text);
```

Example 16. Harder substitution

```
//urlify - turn URLs into HTML links
$text = "Check the web site, http://www.oreilly.com/catalog/
regexppr.";
$regex =
        "{ \\b                      # start at word\n"
      . "                           # boundary\n"
      . "(                          # capture to $1\n"
      . "(https?|telnet|gopher|file|wais|ftp) : \n"
      . "                           # resource and colon\n"
      . "[\\w/\\#~:.?+=&%@!\\-]+?    # one or more valid\n"
      . "                           # characters\n"
      . "                           # but take as little as\n"
      . "                           # possible\n"
      . ")\n"
      . "(?=                        # lookahead\n"
      . "[.:?\\-]*                   # for possible punct\n"
      . "(?:[^\\w/\\#~:.?+=&%@!\\-]  # invalid character\n"
      . "|$)                        # or end of string\n"
      . ") }x";


echo preg_replace($regex, "<a href=\"$1\">$1</a>", $text);
```

Other Resources

- PHP's online documentation at *http://www.php.net/pcre*.
- *Mastering Regular Expressions*, Third Edition, by Jeffrey E. F. Friedl (O'Reilly), covers the details of PHP regular expressions on pages 439–481.

Python

Python provides a rich, Perl-like regular expression syntax in the re module. The re module uses a Traditional NFA match engine. For an explanation of the rules behind an NFA engine, see "Introduction to Regexes and Pattern Matching."

This chapter will cover the version of re included with Python 2.3.5, although the module has been available in similar form since Python 1.5.

Supported Metacharacters

The re module supports the metacharacters and metasequences listed in Table 27 through Table 31. For expanded definitions of each metacharacter, see "Regex Metacharacters, Modes, and Constructs."

Table 27. Python character representations

Sequence	Meaning
\a	Alert (bell), \x07.
\b	Backspace, \x08, supported only in character class.
\n	Newline, \x0A.
\r	Carriage return, \x0D.
\f	Form feed, \x0C.
\t	Horizontal tab, \x09.
\v	Vertical tab, \x0B.
\octal	Character specified by up to three octal digits.

Table 27. Python character representations (continued)

Sequence	Meaning
\x*hh*	Character specified by a two-digit hexadecimal code.
\u*hhhh*	Character specified by a four-digit hexadecimal code.
\U*hhhhhhhh*	Character specified by an eight-digit hexadecimal code.

Table 28. Python character classes and class-like constructs

Class	Meaning
[...]	Any character listed, or contained within a listed range.
[^...]	Any character that is not listed, and is not contained within a listed range.
.	Any character, except a newline (unless DOTALL mode).
\w	Word character, [a-zA-z0-9_] (unless LOCALE or UNICODE mode).
\W	Nonword character, [^a-zA-z0-9_] (unless LOCALE or UNICODE mode).
\d	Digit character, [0-9].
\D	Nondigit character, [^0-9].
\s	Whitespace character, [\t\n\r\f\v].
\S	Nonwhitespace character, [\t\n\r\f\v].

Table 29. Python anchors and zero-width tests

Sequence	Meaning
^	Start of string, or the point after any newline if in MULTILINE match mode.
\A	Start of search string, in all match modes.
$	End of search string, or the point before a string-ending newline, or before any newline in MULTILINE match mode.
\Z	End of string, or the point before a string-ending newline, in any match mode.
\b	Word boundary.
\B	Not-word-boundary.

Table 29. Python anchors and zero-width tests (continued)

Sequence	Meaning
(?=...)	Positive lookahead.
(?!...)	Negative lookahead.
(?<=...)	Positive lookbehind.
(?<!...)	Negative lookbehind.

Table 30. Python comments and mode modifiers

Modifier/sequence	Mode character	Meaning
I or IGNORECASE	i	Case-insensitive matching.
L or LOCALE	L	Cause \w, \W, \b, and \B to use current locale's definition of alphanumeric.
M or MULTILINE or (?m)	m	^ and $ match next to embedded \n.
S or DOTALL or (?s)	s	Dot (.) matches newline.
U or UNICODE or (?u)	u	Cause \w, \W, \b, and \B to use Unicode definition of alphanumeric.
X or VERBOSE or (?x)	x	Ignore whitespace, and allow comments (#) in pattern.
(?mode)		Turn listed modes (one or more of iLmsux) on for the entire regular expression.
(?#...)		Treat substring as a comment.
#...		Treat rest of line as a comment in VERBOSE mode.

Table 31. Python grouping, capturing, conditional, and control

Sequence	Meaning
(...)	Group subpattern, and capture submatch, into \1,\2,....
(?P<name> ...)	Group subpattern, and capture submatch, into named capture group, *name*.

Table 31. Python grouping, capturing, conditional, and control (continued)

Sequence	Meaning
(?P=*name*)	Match text matched by earlier named capture group, *name*.
\n	Contains the results of the *n*th earlier submatch.
(?:...)	Groups subpattern, but does not capture submatch.
...|...	Try subpatterns in alternation.
*	Match 0 or more times.
+	Match 1 or more times.
?	Match 1 or 0 times.
{*n*}	Match exactly *n* times.
{*x*,*y*}	Match at least *x* times, but no more than *y* times.
*?	Match 0 or more times, but as few times as possible.
+?	Match 1 or more times, but as few times as possible.
??	Match 0 or 1 time, but as few times as possible.
{*x*,*y*}?	Match at least *x* times, no more than *y* times, and as few times as possible.

re Module Objects and Functions

The re module defines all regular expression functionality. Pattern matching is done directly through module functions, or patterns are compiled into regular expression objects that can be used for repeated pattern matching. Information about the match, including captured groups, is retrieved through match objects.

Python's raw string syntax, r'' or r"", allows you to specify regular expression patterns without having to escape embedded backslashes. The raw-string pattern, r'\n', is equivalent to the regular string pattern, \\n. Python also provides triple-quoted raw strings for multiline regular expressions: r'''*text*''' and r"""*text*""".

Module Functions

The re module defines the following functions and one exception.

compile(*pattern* [, *flags*])

> Return a regular expression object with the optional mode modifiers, *flags*.

match(*pattern*, *string* [, *flags*])

> Search for *pattern* at starting position of *string*, and return a match object or None if no match.

search(*pattern*, *string* [, *flags*])

> Search for *pattern* in *string*, and return a match object or None if no match.

split(*pattern*, *string* [, *maxsplit=0*])

> Split *string* on *pattern*, and limit the number of splits to *maxsplit*. Submatches from capturing parentheses are also returned.

sub(*pattern*, *repl*, *string* [, *count=0*])

> Return a string with all or up to *count* occurrences of *pattern* in *string* replaced with *repl*. *repl* may be a string, or a function that takes a match object argument.

subn(*pattern*, *repl*, *string* [, *count=0*])

> Perform sub( ), but return a tuple of the new string, and the number of replacements.

findall(*pattern*, *string*)

> Return matches of *pattern* in *string*. If *pattern* has capturing groups, returns a list of submatches, or a list of tuples of submatches.

finditer(*pattern*, *string*)

> Return an iterator over matches of *pattern* in *string*. For each match, the iterator returns a match object.

escape(*string*)

> Return the string with alphanumerics backslashed so that *string* can be matched literally.

exception error

> The exception raised if an error occurs during compilation or matching. This is common if a string passed to a function is not a valid regular expression.

RegExp

Regular expression objects are created with the `re.compile` function.

flags
>   Return the flags argument used when the object was compiled, or 0.

groupindex
>   Return a dictionary that maps symbolic group names to group numbers.

pattern
>   Return the pattern string used when the object was compiled.

match(*string [, pos [, endpos]]*)

search(*string [, pos [, endpos]]*)

split(*string [, maxsplit=0]*)

sub(*repl, string [, count=0]*)

subn(*repl, string [, count=0]*)

findall(*string*)
>   Same as the re module functions, except `pattern` is implied. *pos* and *endpos* give start and end string indexes for the match.

Match Objects

Match objects are created by the `match` and `find` functions.

pos

endpos
>   Value of pos or endpos passed to `search` or `match`.

re
>   The regular expression object whose `match` or `search` returned this object.

string
>   String passed to `match` or `search`.

group([*g1, g2, ...*])
>   Return one or more submatches from capturing groups. Groups may be numbers corresponding to capturing groups, or strings corresponding to named capturing groups. Group 0

corresponds to the entire match. If no arguments are provided, this function returns the entire match. Capturing groups that did not match have a result of None.

groups([*default*])

Return a tuple of the results of all capturing groups. Groups that did not match have the value None or *default*.

groupdict([*default*])

Return a dictionary of named capture groups, keyed by group name. Groups that did not match have the value None or *default*.

start([*group*])

Index of start of substring matched by *group* (or start of entire matched string if no *group*).

end([*group*])

Index of end of substring matched by *group* (or end of entire matched string if no *group*).

span([*group*])

Return a tuple of starting and ending indexes of *group* (or matched string if no *group*).

expand([*template*])

Return a string obtained by doing backslash substitution on *template*. Character escapes, numeric backreferences, and named backreferences are expanded.

lastgroup

Name of the last matching capture group, or None if no match or if the group had no name.

lastindex

Index of the last matching capture group, or None if no match.

Unicode Support

re provides limited Unicode support. Strings may contain Unicode characters, and individual Unicode characters can be specified with \u. Additionally, the UNICODE flag causes \w, \W, \b, and \B to recognize all Unicode alphanumerics. However, re does not provide support for matching Unicode properties, blocks, or categories.

Examples

Example 17. Simple match

```
#Find Spider-Man, Spiderman, SPIDER-MAN, etc.
import re

dailybugle = 'Spider-Man Menaces City!'
pattern    = r'spider[- ]?man.'

if re.match(pattern, dailybugle, re.IGNORECASE):
    print dailybugle
```

Example 18. Match and capture group

```
#Match dates formatted like MM/DD/YYYY, MM-DD-YY,...
import re

date = '12/30/1969'

regex = re.compile(r'^(\d\d)[-/](\d\d)[-/](\d\d(?:\d\d)?)$')

match = regex.match(date)

if match:
    month = match.group(1) #12
    day   = match.group(2) #30
    year  = match.group(3) #1969
```

Example 19. Simple substitution

```
#Convert <br> to <br /> for XHTML compliance
import re

text  = 'Hello world. <br>'
regex = re.compile(r'<br>', re.IGNORECASE);
repl  = r'<br />'

result = regex.sub(repl,text)
```

Example 20. Harder substitution

```
#urlify - turn URLs into HTML links
import re

text = 'Check the web site, http://www.oreilly.com/catalog/
regexppr.'

pattern =  r'''
     \b                        # start at word boundary
     (                         # capture to \1
     (https?|telnet|gopher|file|wais|ftp) :
                               # resource and colon
     [\w/#~:.?+=&%@!\-] +?      # one or more valid chars
                               # take little as possible
     )
     (?=                       # lookahead
     [.:?\-] *                 #  for possible punc
     (?: [^\w/#~:.?+=&%@!\-]    #  invalid character
     | $ )                     #  or end of string
     )'''

regex = re.compile(pattern,  re.IGNORECASE
                           + re.VERBOSE)

result = regex.sub(r'<a href="\1">\1</a>', text)
```

Other Resources

- Python's online documentation at *http://www.python.org/doc/current/lib/module-re.html*.

RUBY

Ruby provides a subset of Perl-style regular expressions built into the Regexp and String classes. Ruby uses a Traditional NFA match engine. For an explanation of the rules behind a Traditional NFA engine, see "Introduction to Regexes and Pattern Matching."

Ruby 1.9 introduces a new regular expression engine that includes several new features. These features are available in earlier releases as part of the Oniguruma library. The following reference primarily covers Ruby 1.8.6, but the most prominent Ruby 1.9 features are also included and marked.

Supported Metacharacters

Ruby supports the metacharacters and metasequences listed in Table 32 through Table 37. For expanded definitions of each metacharacter, see "Regex Metacharacters, Modes, and Constructs."

Table 32. Ruby character representations

Sequence	Meaning
\a	Alert (bell), \x07.
\b	Backspace, \x08, supported only in character class.
\e	ESC character, \x1B.
\n	Newline, \x0A.
\r	Carriage return, \x0D.
\f	Form feed, \x0C.
\t	Horizontal tab, \x09.
\v	Vertical tab, \x0B.
\0*octal*	Character specified by a two-digit octal code.
\x*hex*	Character specified by a two-digit hexadecimal code.
\c*char*	Named control character.

Table 33. Ruby character classes and class-like constructs

Class	Meaning
[...]	A single character listed, or contained within a listed range.
[^...]	A single character not listed, and not contained within a listed range.

Table 33. Ruby character classes and class-like constructs (continued)

Class	Meaning
.	Any character, except a line terminator (unless single-line mode, s).
\w	Word character.
\W	Nonword character.
\d	Digit.
\D	Nondigit.
\s	Whitespace character, [\f\n\r\t\v].
\S	Nonwhitespace character, [^ \f\n\r\t\v].

Table 34. Ruby anchors and other zero-width tests

Sequence	Meaning
^	Start of string, or the point after any newline.
\A	Beginning of string, in all match modes.
$	End of string, or the point before any newline.
\Z	End of string, but before any final line terminator, in all match modes.
\z	End of string, in all match modes.
\b	Boundary between a \w character and a \W character.
\B	Not-word-boundary.
\G	End of the previous match.
(?=...)	Positive lookahead.
(?!...)	Negative lookahead.

Table 35. Ruby comments and mode modifiers

Mode character	Meaning
m	Dot (.) matches any character, including a line terminator. Note that this is different from most regex implementations.
x	Ignore whitespace, and allow embedded comments starting with #.

Table 35. Ruby comments and mode modifiers (continued)

Mode character	Meaning
i	Case-insensitive match based on characters in the current culture.
n	Turn off wide-character processing.
o	Evaluate #{...} substitutions only once. Default is to evaluate each time the regex is evaluated.
(?imns-imns)	Turn match flags on or off for the rest of pattern.
(?imns-imns: ...)	Turn match flags on or off for the rest of the subexpression.
(?#...)	Treat substring as a comment.
#...	Treat rest of line as a comment in /x mode.
(?<=...)	Positive lookbehind. (Ruby 1.9)
(?<!...)	Negative lookbehind. (Ruby 1.9)

Table 36. Ruby grouping, capturing, conditional, and control

Sequence	Meaning
(...)	Grouping. Submatches fill \1, \2,... and $1, $2,....
(?<name>...)	Named captured. Grouped match will fill \k<name>. (Ruby 1.9)
\n	In a regular expression, match what was matched by the nth earlier submatch.
$n	In a replacement string, contains the nth earlier submatch.
\k<name>	In a replacement string, contains the named submatch name. (Ruby 1.9)
(?:...)	Grouping-only parentheses, no capturing.
(?>...)	Atomic grouping.
...|...	Alternation; match one or the other.
*	Match 0 or more times.
+	Match 1 or more times.
?	Match 1 or 0 times.
{n}	Match exactly n times.

Table 36. Ruby grouping, capturing, conditional, and control (continued)

Sequence	Meaning
{n,}	Match at least *n* times.
{x,y}	Match at least *x* times, but no more than *y* times.
*?	Match 0 or more times, but as few times as possible.
+?	Match 1 or more times, but as few times as possible.
??	Match 0 or 1 times, but as few times as possible.
{n,}?	Match at least *n* times, but as few times as possible.
{x,y}?	Match at least *x* times, no more than *y* times, and as few times as possible.

Table 37. Ruby replacement sequences

Sequence	Meaning
$1, $2, ...	Captured submatches.
${name}	Matched text of a named capture group.
$'	Text before match.
$&	Text of match.
$`	Text after match.
$+	Last parenthesized match.

Object-Oriented Interface

Ruby provides an object-oriented regular expression interface through the Regexp and MatchData classes, as well as several built-in methods of the String class.

Ruby also provides the /.../ and =~ operators to provide a Perl-like operator syntax. The /.../ operator is a synonym for Regexp.new, and =~ is a synonym for String#match. The /.../ operator is commonly used to pass a Regexp object to a method, e.g., "foo, bar, frog".split(/,\s*/).

String

Description
String objects contain built-in methods for regular expression pattern matching and substitution, as well as several methods for string manipulation that take regular expressions as arguments.

Instance Methods

string =~ *regexp* => fixnum or nil
> Match the *regexp*, and return the position that the match starts, or nil.

regexp === *string* => boolean
> Return true if the regexp matches the string. Used in case-when statements.

gsub(*pattern*, *replacement*) => new_string

gsub(*pattern*) {|match| block } => new_string
> Return a copy of string with all occurrences of *pattern* replaced with *replacement*, or the value of the block. Otherwise, behaves as Regexp#sub.

gsub!(pattern, replacement) => string or nil

gsub!(pattern) {|match| block } => string or nil
> Perform the substitutions of String#gsub in place, returning string or returning nil if no substitutions were performed.

index(*regexp* [, *offset*]) => fixnum or nil
> Return the index of the first match by *regexp* or nil if not found. Optionally, *offset* specifies the position in the string to begin the search.

match(pattern) => matchdata or nil
> Apply a regex *pattern* or Regexp object to the string, returning a MatchData object, or returning nil if there was no match.

rindex(*regexp* [, fixnum]) => fixnum or nil
> Return the index of the first match by *regexp* or nil if not found. Optionally, *offset* specifies the position in the string to end the search; characters to the right of this point will not be considered.

scan(regexp) => array

scan(*regexp*) {|match, ...| block } => string

Iterate through the string, and return either an array of matches, or, if the *regexp* contains matching groups, an array of arrays.

[regexp] => substring or nil

[regexp, *fixnum*] => substring or nil

slice(regexp) => substring or nil

slice(regexp, *fixnum*) => substring or nil

Return the matched substring or nil. If a *fixnum* is provided, return the corresponding submatch.

slice!(regexp) => new_str or nil

Delete the matching portion of the string, and return the portion deleted, or return nil if there is no match.

split(pattern=$;, [*limit*]) => anArray

Divides the string into substrings based on a delimiter, which can be either a string, or a Regexp object.

If *limit* is positive, returns at most *limit* matches. If no *limit* is provided, trailing empty substrings are omitted. If *limit* is negative, all substrings are returned, including trailing empty substrings.

sub(*regexp*, *replacement*) => new_string

sub(*regexp*) {|match| block } => new_string

Return a copy of the string with the first match of *regexp* replaced with *replacement*, or the value of the block. The *replacement* string may reference submatches with the sequences \1, \2, ..., *n*. The block form can reference the special match variables $1, $2, $`, $&, and $´.

sub!(pattern, replacement) => string or nil

sub!(pattern) {|match| block } => string or nil

Performs the substitutions of String#sub in place, returning *string*, or returning nil if no substitutions were performed.

Regexp

Description

Holds a regular expression that is used to match a pattern against strings.

Class Methods

escape(string) => escaped_string

quote(string) => escaped_string
> Escape regular expression metacharacters, so they aren't interpreted when used inside a regular expression pattern.

last_match => matchdata

last_match(n) => string
> Return the MatchData of the last successful match, or the *n*th field in the MatchData object.

Regexp.new(pattern [, options [, lang]]) => regexp

Regexp.compile(pattern [, options [, lang]]) => regexp
> Create a new Regexp object from a regular expression pattern. Options can be an OR'd combination of Regexp::EXTENDED, Regexp::IGNORECASE, and Regexp::MULTILINE. The lang parameter enables multibyte support for the regexp: 'n', 'N' = none, 'e', 'E' = EUC, 's', 'S' = SJIS, 'u', 'U' = UTF-8.

Regexp.union([pattern]*) => new_str
> Create a Regexp object that is the union of given patterns joined by the alternation operator, where each pattern is either a pattern string, or a Regexp object.

Instance Methods

regexp == second_regexp => boolean

regexp.eql?(second_regexp) => boolean
> Return true if two Regexp objects are based on identical patterns, and have the same character set code and mode options.

match(string) => matchdata or nil
> Return a MatchData object describing the match, or nil if there was no match.

casefold? => true or false
> Return true if IGNORECASE is set for the entire pattern.

inspect => string
> Return a string representation of the Regexp object.

kcode => string
> Return the character set code for the Regexp object.

options => fixnum
> Return the set of bits corresponding to the options used when creating this Regexp. These bits can be passed as the options to a new Regexp.

---

source => string
> Return the original pattern string.

to_s => string
> Return a string containing the regular expression, and its options, using the (?imns-imns:...) notation.

MatchData

Description

Holds the results of a successful match, including the matched string, and submatches from match groups.

Instance Methods

[i] => string

[start, length] => array

[range] => array
> Access match results as an array. Element 0 is the entire matched string, and elements 1 through *n* contain submatches.

begin(n) => integer
> Return the offset of the start of the *n*th submatch in the string.

captures => array
> Return the array of captures, equivalent to MatchData#to_a.

end(n) => integer
> Return the offset of the end of the *n*th submatch in the string.

length => integer

size => integer
> Return the number of elements, including the full match and submatches, in the match array.

offset(n) => array
> Return a two-element array containing the beginning and ending offsets of the *n*th submatch.

post_match => string
> Return the portion of the original string after the current match (same as $`).

pre_match => string
> Return the portion of the original string before the current match (same as $`).

```
select([index]*) => array
```
Use each index to access the submatches, returning an array of the corresponding values.
```
string => original_string
```
Return a copy of the string passed in to match.
```
to_a => anArray
```
Return the array of matches.
```
to_s => string
```
Return the entire matched string.

Unicode Support

Ruby has some UTF-8 support, but you have to enable it by including the line $KCODE = "UTF8" before using the constructs. When enabled, the metasequences \w, \d, \s, and \b support Unicode characters outside of the ASCII range. You can also enable multibyte regex processing by passing a language parameter to Regexp.new, and turn off multibyte processing with the /n modifier.

Examples

Example 21. Simple match

```
#Find Spider-Man, Spiderman, SPIDER-MAN, etc.

dailybugle = 'Spider-Man Menaces City!'

if dailybugle.match(/spider[- ]?man./i)
    puts dailybugle
end
```

Example 22. Match and capture group

```
#Match dates formatted like MM/DD/YYYY, MM-DD-YY,...

date = '12/30/1969'

regexp = Regexp.new('^(\d\d)[-/](\d\d)[-/](\d\d(?:\d\d)?)$')
```

Example 22. Match and capture group (continued)

```
if md = regexp.match(date)
  month = md[1] #12
  day   = md[2] #30
  year  = md[3] #1969
end
```

Example 23. Simple substitution

```
#Convert <br> to <br /> for XHTML compliance

text = 'Hello world. <br>'
regexp = Regexp.new('<br>', Regexp::IGNORECASE)

result = text.sub(regexp, "<br />")
```

Example 24. Harder substitution

```
#urlify - turn URLs into HTML links
text = 'Check the web site, http://www.oreilly.com/catalog/
regexppr.'

regexp = Regexp.new('
     \b                          # start at word boundary
       (                         # capture to \1
       (https?|telnet|gopher|file|wais|ftp) :
                                 # resource and colon
       [\w/#~:.?+=&%@!\-] +?     # one or more valid chars
                                 # take little as possible
       )
       (?=                       # lookahead
       [.:?\-] *                 # for possible punc
       (?: [^\w/#~:.?+=&%@!\-]   # invalid character
       | $ )                     # or end of string
       )', Regexp::EXTENDED)


result = text.sub(regexp, '<a href="\1">\1</a>')
```

JavaScript

JavaScript introduced Perl-like regular expression support with version 1.2. This reference covers versions 1.5 through 1.7 as defined by the ECMA standard. Supporting implementations include Microsoft Internet Explorer 5.5+ and Firefox 1.0++. JavaScript uses a Traditional NFA match engine. For an explanation of the rules behind this NFA engine, see "Introduction to Regexes and Pattern Matching."

Supported Metacharacters

JavaScript supports the metacharacters and metasequences listed in Table 38 through Table 42. For expanded definitions of each metacharacter, see "Regex Metacharacters, Modes, and Constructs."

Table 38. JavaScript character representations

Sequence	Meaning
\0	Null character, \x00.
\b	Backspace, \x08; supported only in character class.
\n	Newline, \x0A.
\r	Carriage return, \x0D.
\f	Form feed, \x0C.
\t	Horizontal tab, \x09.
\t	Vertical tab, \x0B.
\xhh	Character specified by a two-digit hexadecimal code.
\uhhhh	Character specified by a four-digit hexadecimal code.
\cchar	Named control character.

Table 39. JavaScript character classes and class-like constructs

Class	Meaning
[...]	A single character listed, or contained within a listed range.
[^...]	A single character not listed, and not contained within a listed range.
.	Any character except a line terminator, [^\x0A\x0D\u2028\u2029].
\w	Word character, [a-zA-Z0-9_].
\W	Nonword character, [^a-zA-Z0-9_].
\d	Digit character, [0-9].
\D	Nondigit character, [^0-9].
\s	Whitespace character.
\S	Nonwhitespace character.

Table 40. JavaScript anchors and other zero-width tests

Sequence	Meaning
^	Start of string, or the point after any newline if in multiline match mode, /m.
$	End of search string, or the point before a string-ending newline, or before any newline if in multiline match mode, /m.
\b	Word boundary.
\B	Not-word-boundary.
(?=...)	Positive lookahead.
(?!...)	Negative lookahead.

Table 41. JavaScript mode modifiers

Modifier	Meaning
m	^ and $ match next to embedded line terminators.
i	Case-insensitive match.

Table 42. JavaScript grouping, capturing, conditional, and control

Sequence	Meaning
(...)	Group subpattern, and capture submatch, into \1, \2, ... and $1, $2, ...
\n	In a regular expression, contains text matched by the *n*th capture group.
$n	In a replacement string, contains text matched by the *n*th capture group.
(?:...)	Group subpattern, but do not capture submatch.
...|...	Try subpatterns in alternation.
*	Match 0 or more times.
+	Match 1 or more times.
?	Match 1 or 0 times.
{n}	Match exactly *n* times.
{n,}	Match at least *n* times.
{x,y}	Match at least *x* times, but no more than *y* times.
*?	Match 0 or more times, but as few times as possible.
+?	Match 1 or more times, but as few times as possible.
??	Match 0 or 1 time, but as few times as possible.
{n}?	Match at least *n* times, but as few times as possible.
{x,y}?	Match at least *x* times, no more than *y* times, and as few times as possible.

Pattern-Matching Methods and Objects

JavaScript provides convenient pattern-matching methods in String objects, as well as a RegExp object for more complex pattern matching. JavaScript strings use the backslash for escapes; therefore, any escapes destined for the regular expression engine should be double escaped (e.g., \\w instead of \w). You can also use the regular expression literal syntax, /pattern/img.

String

Strings support four convenience methods for pattern matching. Each method takes a *pattern* argument, which may be a RegExp object, or a string containing a regular expression pattern.

Methods

search(*pattern*)

> Match *pattern* against the string, returning either the character position of the start of the first matching substring or -1.

replace(*pattern*, *replacement*)

> Search the string for a match of *pattern*, and replace the matched substring with *replacement*. If *pattern* has global mode set, all matches of *pattern* are replaced. The replacement string may have n constructs that are replaced with the matched text of the *n*th capture group in *pattern*.

match(*pattern*)

> Match *pattern* against the string, returning either an array or -1. Element 0 of the array contains the full match. Additional elements contain submatches from capture groups. In global (g) mode, the array contains all matches of *pattern* with no capture group submatches.

split(*pattern*, *limit*)

> Return an array of strings broken around *pattern*. If *limit* is included, the array contains at most the first *limit* substrings broken around *pattern*. If *pattern* contains capture groups, captured substrings are returned as elements after each split substring.

RegExp

Models a regular expression, and contains methods for pattern matching.

Constructor

new RegExp(*pattern*, *attributes*)

/*pattern*/*attributes*

> RegExp objects can be created with either the RegExp( ) constructor, or a special literal syntax /.../. The parameter *pattern* is a required regular expression pattern, and the

parameter *attributes* is an optional string containing any of the mode modifiers g, i, or m. The parameter *pattern* can also be a RegExp object, but then the *attributes* parameter becomes required.

The constructor can throw two exceptions. SyntaxError is thrown if *pattern* is malformed, or if *attributes* contains invalid mode modifiers. *TypeError* is thrown if *pattern* is a RegExp object, and the *attributes* parameter is omitted.

Instance properties

global
> Boolean indicating whether RegExp has g attribute.

ignoreCase
> Boolean indicating whether RegExp has i attribute.

lastIndex
> The character position of the last match.

multiline
> Boolean indicating whether RegExp has m attribute.

source
> The text pattern used to create this object.

Methods

exec(*text*)
> Search *text*, and return an array of strings if the search succeeds, and null if it fails. Element 0 of the array contains the substring matched by the entire regular expression. Additional elements correspond to capture groups.
>
> If the global flag (g) is set, then lastIndex is set to the character position after the match, or zero if there was no match. Successive exec( ) or test( ) calls will start at lastIndex. Note that lastIndex is a property of the regular expression, not the string being searched. You must reset lastIndex manually if you are using a RegExp object in global mode to search multiple strings.

test(*text*)
> Return true if the RegExp object matches *text*. The test( ) method behaves in the same way as exec( ) when used in global mode: successive calls start at lastIndex, even if used on different strings.

Examples

Example 25. Simple match

```
//Find Spider-Man, Spiderman, SPIDER-MAN, etc.
    var dailybugle = "Spider-Man Menaces City!";

    //regex must match entire string
    var regex = /spider[- ]?man/i;

    if (dailybugle.search(regex)) {
      //do something
    }
```

Example 26. Match and capture group

```
//Match dates formatted like MM/DD/YYYY, MM-DD-YY,...
    var date = "12/30/1969";
    var p =
      new RegExp("^(\\d\\d)[-/](\\d\\d)[-/](\\d\\d\\d(?:\\d\\
d)?)$");

    var result = p.exec(date);
    if (result != null) {
      var month = result[1];
      var day   = result[2];
      var year  = result[3];
```

Example 27. Simple substitution

```
//Convert <br> to <br /> for XHTML compliance
    String text = "Hello world. <br>";

    var pattern = /<br>/ig;

    test.replace(pattern, "<br />");
```

Example 28. Harder substitution

```
//urlify - turn URLs into HTML links
   var text = "Check the web site, http://www.oreilly.com/
catalog/regexppr.";
   var regex =
        "\\b"                       // start at word boundary
     + "("                          // capture to $1
```

Example 28. Harder substitution (continued)

```
+   "(https?|telnet|gopher|file|wais|ftp) :"
                                    // resource and colon
+   "[\\w/\\#~:.?+=&%@!\\-]+?"   // one or more valid chars
                                    // take little as possible
+   ")"
+   "(?="                           // lookahead
+   "[.:?\\-]*"                    // for possible punct
+   "(?:[^\\w/\\#~:.?+=&%@!\\-]"// invalid character
+   "|$)"                           // or end of string
+   ")";

text.replace(regex, "<a href=\"$1\">$1</a>");
```

Other Resources

- *JavaScript: The Definitive Guide*, by David Flanagan
  (O'Reilly), is a reference for all JavaScript, including
  regular expressions.

PCRE

The Perl Compatible Regular Expression (PCRE) library is a
free-for-any-use, open source, C-language regular expression
library developed by Philip Hazel. PCRE has been incorpo-
rated into PHP, the Apache web server 2.0, KDE, Exim,
Analog, and Postfix. Users of those programs can use the supported metacharacters listed in Table 43 through Table 47.

The PCRE library uses a Traditional NFA match engine. For
an explanation of the rules behind an NFA engine, see
"Introduction to Regexes and Pattern Matching."

This reference covers PCRE Version 7.0, which aims to emu-
late Perl 5.8-style regular expressions, but also includes
features from the upcoming Perl 5.10.

PCRE can be compiled with or without support for UTF-8
strings, and with or without support for Unicode character
properties. The following lists and tables assume that both
these features are available.

Supported Metacharacters

PCRE supports the metacharacters and metasequences listed in Table 43 through Table 47. For expanded definitions of each metacharacter, see "Regex Metacharacters, Modes, and Constructs."

Table 43. PCRE character representations

Sequence	Meaning
\a	Alert (bell), \x07.
\b	Backspace, \x08; supported only in character class.
\e	Escape character, \x1B.
\n	Newline, \x0A.
\r	Carriage return, \x0D.
\f	Form feed, \x0C.
\t	Horizontal tab, \x09.
\octal	Character specified by a three-digit octal code.
\xhex	Character specified by a one- or two-digit hexadecimal code.
\x{hex}	Character specified by any hexadecimal code.
\cchar	Named control character.
\p{prop}	Character contained by given Unicode block or property.
\P{prop}	Character not contained by given Unicode block or property.

Table 44. PCRE character classes and class-like constructs

Class	Meaning
[...]	A single character listed, or contained in a listed range.
[^...]	A single character not listed, and not contained within a listed range.
[:class:]	POSIX-style character class valid only within a regex character class.
.	Any character, except newline (unless single-line mode, PCRE_DOTALL).

Table 44. PCRE character classes and class-like constructs

Class	Meaning
\C	One byte; however, this may corrupt a Unicode character stream.
\w	Word character, [a-zA-z0-9_].
\W	Nonword character, [^a-zA-z0-9_].
\d	Digit character, [0-9].
\D	Nondigit character, [^0-9].
\s	Whitespace character, [\n\r\f\t\v].
\S	Nonwhitespace character, [^\n\r\f\t\v].
\R	Unicode newline sequence.

Table 45. PCRE anchors and zero-width tests

Sequence	Meaning
^	Start of string, or the point after any newline if in multiline match mode, PCRE_MULTILINE.
\A	Start of search string, in all match modes.
$	End of search string, or the point before a string-ending newline, or before any newline if in multiline match mode, PCRE_MULTILINE.
\Z	End of string, or the point before a string-ending newline, in any match mode.
\z	End of string, in any match mode.
\G	Beginning of current search.
\b	Word boundary; position between a word character (\w) and a nonword character (\W), the start of the string, or the end of the string.
\B	Not-word-boundary.
(?=...)	Positive lookahead.
(?!...)	Negative lookahead.
(?<=...)	Positive lookbehind.
(?<!...)	Negative lookbehind.

Table 46. PCRE comments and mode modifiers

Modifier/sequence	Equivalent Perl mode character	Meaning
PCRE_CASELESS	i	Case-insensitive matching for characters with codepoints values less than 256. In UTF-8 mode, it works for all characters if Unicode property support is available.
PCRE_MULTILINE	m	^ and $ match next to embedded \n.
PCRE_DOTALL	s	Dot (.) matches newline.
PCRE_EXTENDED	x	Ignore whitespace, and allow comments (#) in pattern.
PCRE_UNGREEDY	U	Reverse greediness of all quantifiers: * becomes nongreedy, and *? becomes greedy.
PCRE_ANCHORED		Force match to start at the first position searched.
PCRE_DOLLAR_ENDONLY		Force $ to match at only the end of a string instead of before a string ending with a newline. Overridden by multiline mode.
PCRE_NO_AUTO_CAPTURE		Disable capturing function of parentheses.
PCRE_UTF8		Treat regular expression and subject strings as strings of multibyte UTF-8 characters.
PCRE_AUTO_CALLOUT		Insert automatic callouts.
PCRE_DUPNAMES		Allow duplicate named groups.
PCRE_FIRSTLINE		Unanchored pattern must match before the first newline of the subject.
PCRE_NEWLINE_CR PCRE_NEWLINE_LF PCRE_NEWLINE_CRLF PCRE_NEWLINE_ANY		Specify newline character sequence.
PCRE_NOTBOL		Start of subject is not start of line.
PCRE_NOTEOL		End of subject is not end of line.

Table 46. PCRE comments and mode modifiers (continued)

Modifier/sequence	Equivalent Perl mode character	Meaning
PCRE_NOTEMPTY		An empty string is not a valid match.
PCRE_NO_UTF8_CHECK		Do not validate UTF-8 strings.
PCRE_PARTIAL		Failed matches that reach the end of the input string return PCRE_ PARTIAL rather than PCRE_ ERROR_NO_MATCH.
(?mode)		Turn listed modes (one or more of imsxU) on for the rest of the subexpression.
(?-mode)		Turn listed modes (one or more of imsxU) off for the rest of the subexpression.
(?mode:...)		Turn listed modes (one or more of imsx) on within parentheses.
(?-mode:...)		Turn listed modes (one or more of imsx) off within parentheses.
\Q		Quote all following regex metacharacters.
\E		End a span started with \Q.
(?#...)		Treat substring as a comment.
#...		Treat rest of line as a comment in PCRE_EXTENDED mode.

Table 47. PCRE grouping, capturing, conditional, and control

Sequence	Meaning
(...)	Group subpattern and capture submatch into \1,\2,....
(?P<name>...), (?<name>),(?'name')	Group subpattern and capture submatch into named capture group, *name*.
(?P=name),\k<name>, \k'name'	Backreference to named capture.
\n, \gn, \g{n}	Contains the results of the *n*th earlier submatch from a parentheses capture group or a named capture group.

Table 47. PCRE grouping, capturing, conditional,
and control (continued)

Sequence	Meaning
(?:...)	Group subpattern, but do not capture submatch.
(?>...)	Atomic grouping.
...|...	Try subpatterns in alternation.
*	Match 0 or more times.
+	Match 1 or more times.
?	Match 1 or 0 times.
{n}	Match exactly n times.
{n,}	Match at least n times.
{x,y}	Match at least x times, but no more than y times.
*?	Match 0 or more times, but as few times as possible.
+?	Match 1 or more times, but as few times as possible.
??	Match 0 or 1 times, but as few times as possible.
{n,}?	Match at least n times, but as few times as possible.
{x,y}?	Match at least x times, no more than y times, and as few times as possible.
*+	Match 0 or more times, and never backtrack.
++	Match 1 or more times, and never backtrack.
?+	Match 0 or 1 times, and never backtrack.
{n}+	Match at least n times, and never backtrack.
{n,}+	Match at least n times, and never backtrack.
{x,y}+	Match at least x times, no more than y times, and never backtrack.

*Table 47. PCRE grouping, capturing, conditional,
and control (continued)*

Sequence	Meaning
`(?(condition)...|...)`	Match with if-then-else pattern. The *condition* can be either the number of a capture group, or a lookahead or lookbehind construct.
`(?(condition)...)`	Match with if-then pattern. The *condition* can be either the number of a capture group, or a lookahead or lookbehind construct.

PCRE API

Applications using PCRE should look for the API prototypes in pcre.h, and include the actual library file, libpcre.a, by compiling with -lpcre.

Most functionality is contained in the functions pcre_compile( ), which prepares a regular expression data structure, and pcre_exec( ), which performs the pattern matching. You are responsible for freeing memory, although PCRE does provide pcre_free_substring( ) and pcre_free_substring_list( ) to help out.

PCRE API Synopsis

pcre *pcre_compile(const char *pattern, int options, const char **errptr, int *erroffset, const unsigned char *tableptr)

> Compile *pattern* with optional mode modifiers *options*, and optional locale tables *tableptr*, which are created with pcre_maketables( ). Returns a compiled regex, or NULL, with *errptr* pointing to an error message, and *erroffset* pointing to the position in *pattern* where the error occurred.

int pcre_exec(const pcre *code, const pcre_extra *extra, const char *subject, int length, int startoffset, int options, int *ovector, int ovecsize)

> Perform pattern matching with a compiled regular expression, *code*, and a supplied input string, *subject*, of length *length*. The results of a successful match are stored in *ovector*. The first and second elements of *ovector* contain the

position of the first character in the overall match, and the character following the end of the overall match. Each additional pair of elements, up to two-thirds the length of *ovector*, contain the positions of the starting character, and the character after capture group submatches. Optional parameters *options* contain mode modifiers, and pcre_extra contains the results of a call to pcre_study().

pcre_extra *pcre_study(const pcre *code, int options, const char **errptr)

> Return information to speed up calls to pcre_exec() with *code*. There are currently no options, so *options* should always be 0. If an error occurred, *errptr* points to an error message.

int pcre_copy_named_substring(const pcre *code, const char *subject, int *ovector, int stringcount, const char *stringname, char *buffer, int buffersize)

> Copy the substring matched by the named capture group *stringname* into *buffer*. *stringcount* is the number of substrings placed into *ovector*, usually the result returned by pcre_exec().

int pcre_copy_substring(const char *subject, int *ovector, int stringcount, int stringnumber, char *buffer, int buffersize)

> Copy the substring matched by the numbered capture group *stringnumber* into *buffer*. *stringcount* is the number of substrings placed into *ovector*, usually the result returned by pcre_exec().

int pcre_get_named_substring(const pcre *code, const char *subject, int *ovector, int stringcount, const char *stringname, const char **stringptr)

> Create a new string, pointed to by *stringptr*, containing the substring matched by the named capture group *stringname*. Returns the length of the substring. *stringcount* is the number of substrings placed into *ovector*, usually the result returned by pcre_exec().

int pcre_get_stringnumber(const pcre *code, const char *name)

> Return the number of the capture group associated with the named capture group, *name*.

int pcre_get_substring(const char *subject, int *ovector, int stringcount, int stringnumber, const char **stringptr)

> Create a new string, pointed to by *stringptr*, containing the substring matched by the numbered capture group

---

stringnumber. Returns the length of the substring. *stringcount* is the number of substrings placed into *ovector*, usually the result returned by pcre_exec().

int pcre_get_substring_list(const char *subject*, int *ovector*, int *stringcount*, const char ***listptr*)
> Return a list of pointers, *listptr*, to all captured substrings.

void pcre_free_substring(const char ***stringptr*)
> Free memory pointed to by *stringptr*, and allocated by pcre_get_named_substring( ), or pcre_get_substring_list( ).

void pcre_free_substring_list(const char ****stringptr*)
> Free memory pointed to by *stringptr* and allocated by pcre_get_substring_list( ).

const unsigned char *pcre_maketables(void)
> Build character tables for the current locale.

int pcre_fullinfo(const pcre *code*, const pcre_extra *extra*, int *what*, void *where*)
> Place info on a regex specified by *what* into *where*. Available values for *what* are PCRE_INFO_BACKREFMAX, PCRE_INFO_CAPTURECOUNT, PCRE_INFO_FIRSTBYTE, PCRE_INFO_FIRSTTABLE, PCRE_INFO_LASTLITERAL, PCRE_INFO_NAMECOUNT, PCRE_INFO_NAMEENTRYSIZE, PCRE_INFO_NAMETABLE, PCRE_INFO_OPTIONS, PCRE_INFO_SIZE, and PCRE_INFO_STUDYSIZE.

int pcre_config(int *what*, void *where*)
> Place the value of build-time options specified by *what* into *where*. Available values for *what* are PCRE_CONFIG_UTF8, PCRE_CONFIG_NEWLINE, PCRE_CONFIG_LINK_SIZE, PCRE_CONFIG_POSIX_MALLOC_THRESHOLD, and PCRE_CONFIG_MATCH_LIMIT.

char *pcre_version(void)
> Return a pointer to a string containing the PCRE version and release date.

void *(*pcre_malloc)(size_t)
> Entry point PCRE uses for malloc( ) calls.

void (*pcre_free)(void *)
> Entry point PCRE uses for pcre_free( ) calls.

int (*pcre_callout)(pcre_callout_block *)
> Can be set to a callout function that will be called during matches.

Unicode Support

PCRE provides basic Unicode 5.0 support. When a pattern is compiled with the PCRE_UTF8 flag, the pattern will run on Unicode text. However, PCRE determines case and the property of being a letter or a digit based on a set of default tables. You can supply an alternate set of tables based on a different locale. For example:

```
setlocale(LC_CTYPE, "fr");
tables = pcre_maketables();
re = pcre_compile(..., tables);
```

Examples

Example 29 and Example 30 are adapted from an open source example written by Philip Hazel and copyright by the University of Cambridge, England.

Example 29. Simple match

```
#include <stdio.h>
#include <string.h>
#include <pcre.h>

#define CAPTUREVECTORSIZE 30    /* should be a multiple of 3 */

int main(int argc, char **argv)
{
pcre *regex;
const char *error;
int erroffset;
int capturevector[CAPTUREVECTORSIZE];
int rc;

char *pattern = "spider[- ]?man";
char *text ="SPIDERMAN menaces city!";

/* Compile Regex */
regex = pcre_compile(
  pattern,
  PCRE_CASELESS,  /* OR'd mode modifiers */
```

Example 29. Simple match (continued)

```
  &error,        /* error message */
  &erroffset,    /* position in regex where error occurred */
  NULL);         /* use default locale */

/* Handle Errors */
if (regex = = NULL)
  {
  printf("Compilation failed at offset %d: %s\n", erroffset,
         error);
  return 1;
  }

/* Try Match */
rc = pcre_exec(
  regex,    /* compiled regular expression */
  NULL,     /* optional results from pcre_study */
  text,     /* input string */
  (int)strlen(text), /* length of input string */
  0,        /* starting position in input string */
  0,        /* OR'd options */
  capturevector, /* holds results of capture groups */
  CAPTUREVECTORSIZE);

/* Handle Errors */
if (rc < 0)
  {
  switch(rc)
    {
    case PCRE_ERROR_NOMATCH: printf("No match\n"); break;
    default: printf("Matching error %d\n", rc); break;
    }
  return 1;
  }
return 0;
}
```

Example 30. Match and capture group

```
#include <stdio.h>
#include <string.h>
#include <pcre.h>
```

Example 30. Match and capture group (continued)

```c
#define CAPTUREVECTORSIZE 30   /* should be a multiple of 3 */

int main(int argc, char **argv)
{
pcre *regex;
const char *error;
int erroffset;
int capturevector[CAPTUREVECTORSIZE];
int rc, i;

char *pattern = "(\\d\\d)[-/](\\d\\d)[-/](\\d\\d(?:\\d\\d)?)";
char *text ="12/30/1969";

/* Compile the Regex */
re = pcre_compile(
  pattern,
  PCRE_CASELESS,  /* OR'd mode modifiers */
  &error,         /* error message */
  &erroffset,     /* position in regex where error occurred */
  NULL);          /* use default locale */

/* Handle compilation errors */
if (re = = NULL)
  {
  printf("Compilation failed at offset %d: %s\n",
         erroffset, error);
  return 1;
  }

rc = pcre_exec(
  regex,    /* compiled regular expression */
  NULL,     /* optional results from pcre_study */
  text,     /* input string */
  (int)strlen(text), /* length of input string */
  0,        /* starting position in input string */
  0,        /* OR'd options */
  capturevector, /* holds results of capture groups */
  CAPTUREVECTORSIZE);
```

Example 30. Match and capture group (continued)

```c
/* Handle Match Errors */
if (rc < 0)
  {
  switch(rc)
    {
    case PCRE_ERROR_NOMATCH: printf("No match\n"); break;
    /*
    Handle other special cases if you like
    */
    default: printf("Matching error %d\n", rc); break;
    }
  return 1;
  }

/* Match succeded */

printf("Match succeeded\n");

/* Check for output vector for capture groups */
if (rc = = 0)
  {
  rc = CAPTUREVECTORSIZE/3;
  printf("ovector only has room for %d captured substrings\n",
         rc - 1);
  }

/* Show capture groups */

for (i = 0; i < rc; i++)
  {
  char *substring_start = text + ovector[2*i];
  int substring_length = capturevector[2*i+1]
                         - capturevector[2*i];
  printf("%2d: %.*s\n", i, substring_length, substring_start);
  }

return 0;
}
```

Other Resources

- The C source code and documentation for PCRE at *http://www.pcre.org*.

Apache Web Server

Apache web server 2.0 introduced Perl-style regular expressions based on the PCRE library. Apache 2.2 now has support for PCRE 5.0. The library uses a Traditional NFA match engine. For an explanation of the rules behind an NFA engine, see "Introduction to Regexes and Pattern Matching."

A number of Apache directives work with regular expressions. This section covers Apache 2.2 (which is mostly compatible with 2.0) and the most common directives: RewriteRule, LocationMatch, DirectoryMatch, FilesMatch, ProxyMatch, and AliasMatch.

Supported Metacharacters

Apache supports the metacharacters and metasequences listed in Table 48 through Table 52. For expanded definitions of each metacharacter, see "Regex Metacharacters, Modes, and Constructs."

Table 48. Apache character representations

Sequence	Meaning
octal	Character specified by a three-digit octal code.
\x*hex*	Character specified by a one- or two-digit hexadecimal code.
\x{*hex*}	Character specified by any hexadecimal code.
\c*char*	Named control character.

Table 49. Apache character classes and class-like constructs

Class	Meaning
[...]	A single character listed, or contained within a listed range.
[^...]	A single character not listed, and not contained within a listed range.
[:class:]	POSIX-style character class (valid only within a regex character class).
.	Any character, except newline (unless single-line mode, /s).
\C	One byte; however, this may corrupt a Unicode character stream.
\w	Word character, [a-zA-z0-9_].
\W	Nonword character, [^a-zA-z0-9_].
\d	Digit character, [0-9].
\D	Nondigit character, [^0-9].
\s	Whitespace character, [\n\r\f\t].
\S	Nonwhitespace character, [^\n\r\f\t].

Table 50. Apache anchors and zero-width tests

Sequence	Meaning
^	Start of string.
$	End of search string.
\b	Word boundary; position between a word character (\w) and a nonword character (\W), the start of the string, or the end of the string.
\B	Not-word-boundary.
(?=...)	Positive lookahead.
(?!...)	Negative lookahead.
(?<=...)	Positive lookbehind.
(?<!...)	Negative lookbehind.

Table 51. Apache comments and mode modifiers

Modes	Meaning
NC	Case-insensitive matching.
(?*mode*)	Turn listed modes (one or more of imsxU) on for the rest of the subexpression.
(?-*mode*)	Turn listed modes (one or more of imsxU) off for the rest of the subexpression.
(?*mode*:...)	Turn mode (one of xsmi) on within parentheses.
(?-*mode*:...)	Turn mode (one of xsmi) off within parentheses.
(?#...)	Treat substring as a comment.
#...	Rest of line is treated as a comment in x mode.
\Q	Quotes all following regex metacharacters.
\E	Ends a span started with \Q.

Table 52. Apache grouping, capturing, conditional, and control

Sequence	Meaning
(...)	Group subpattern, and capture submatch into \1, \2....
(?P<*name*>...)	Group subpattern, and capture submatch into named capture group, *name*.
n	Contains the results of the *n*th earlier submatch from a parentheses capture group, or a named capture group.
(?:...)	Groups subpattern, but does not capture submatch.
(?>...)	Atomic grouping.
...|...	Try subpatterns in alternation.
*	Match 0 or more times.
+	Match 1 or more times.
?	Match 1 or 0 times.
{*n*}	Match exactly *n* times.
{*n*,}	Match at least *n* times.
{*x*,*y*}	Match at least *x* times, but no more than *y* times.
*?	Match 0 or more times, but as few times as possible.

Table 52. Apache grouping, capturing, conditional,
and control (continued)

Sequence	Meaning
+?	Match 1 or more times, but as few times as possible.
??	Match 0 or 1 times, but as few times as possible.
{n,}?	Match at least n times, but as few times as possible.
{x,y}?	Match at least x times, no more than y times, and as few times as possible.
*+	Match 0 or more times, and never backtrack.
++	Match 1 or more times, and never backtrack.
?+	Match 0 or 1 times, and never backtrack.
{n}+	Match at least n times, and never backtrack.
{n,}+	Match at least n times, and never backtrack.
{x,y}+	Match at least x times, no more than y times, and never backtrack.
(?(condition)...|...)	Match with if-then-else pattern. The condition can be the number of a capture group, or a lookahead or lookbehind construct.
(?(condition)...)	Match with if-then pattern. The condition can be the number of a capture group, or a lookahead or lookbehind construct.

RewriteRule

The rewrite engine enables regular-expression-based rewriting of URLs. The feature is enabled with the `RewriteEngine On` directive. Most rewrites are a single `RewriteRule`, or a combination of `RewriteCond` directives followed by a `RewriteRule`.

`RewriteRule pattern substitution [[FLAG1, FLAG2, ...]]`
  Rewrites URL to *substitution* if the URL is successfully matched by *pattern*. The *substitution* string can contain back-references (*$N*) to the *RewriteRule* pattern, back-references (*%N*) to the last matched *RewriteCond* pattern, server-variables as in rule condition test-strings (*%{VARNAME}*), and mapping-function calls (*${mapname: key|default}*). Optional flags, listed in Table 53, cause the server to take various actions when a match occurs.

RewriteCond teststring pattern

Define a test condition (Table 54) for applying a *RewriteRule*. Multiple *RewriteCond* directives preceding a *RewriteRule* are combined with an implicit AND, unless specified as OR. The *teststring* can contain back-references (*$N*) to the *RewriteRule* pattern, back-references (*%N*) to the last matched *RewriteCond* pattern, server-variables as in rule condition test-strings (*%{VARNAME}*), and mapping-function calls (*${mapname:key|default}*).

Server variables affecting rewrites are listed in Table 55.

Table 53. Apache RewriteRule flags

Modes	Meaning
C	Chain with next rule. If rule matches, apply the rewrite, and the following chained rewrites; otherwise, stop the chain.
CO=NAME:VAL:domain [:lifetime[:path]]	Set a cookie.
E=VAR:VAL	Set an environment variable.
F	Forbidden; send back 403 code.
G	Gone; send back 401 code.
H=Content-handler	Set the content handler.
L	Last rule; don't apply any more rewrite rules.
N	Next rule; reapply the rewrite rules to the newly rewritten URL.
NC	No case; apply case-insensitive matching.
NE	Disable the application of URL-escaping rules to the output of a rule.
NS	Skip processing if the request is an internal subrequest.
P	Stop rewrite processing, and process the result as an internal proxy request.
PT	Pass through to next handler, setting request structure so that *Alias*, *ScriptAlias*, and *Redirect* can work with the result.
QSA	Append query string.

Table 53. Apache RewriteRule flags (continued)

Modes	Meaning
R[=Code]	Redirect to new URL with optional code. The default code is 302.
S=num	Skip the next num rules.
T=MIME-type	Set the MIME type.

Table 54. Apache RewriteCond flags

Modes	Meaning
NC	No case; apply case-insensitive matching.
OR	Use this to combine rule conditions with a local OR instead of the implicit AND.

Table 55. Apache server variables

HTTP headers	Connection and request
HTTP_USER_AGENT	REMOTE_ADDR
HTTP_REFERER	REMOTE_HOST
HTTP_COOKIE	REMOTE_PORT
HTTP_FORWARDED	REMOTE_USER
HTTP_HOST	REMOTE_IDENT
HTTP_PROXY_CONNECTION	REQUEST_METHOD
HTTP_ACCEPT	SCRIPT_FILENAME
Server internals	PATH_INFO
DOCUMENT_ROOT	AUTH_TYPE
SERVER_ADMIN	**Date and time**
SERVER_ADDR	TIME_YEAR
SERVER_PORT	TIME_MON
SERVER_PROTOCOL	TIME_DAY
SERVER_SOFTWARE	TIME_HOUR

Table 55. *Apache server variables (continued)*

HTTP headers	Connection and request
Specials	TIME_MIN
API_VERSION	*TIME_WDAY*
THE_REQUEST	*TIME*
REQUEST_URI	
REQUEST_FILENAME	
IS_SUBREQ	
HTTPS	

Matching Directives

A number of other Apache directives make use of regular expressions. The following are the most common.

AliasMatch pattern file-path|directory-path
> Map URLs to filesystem locations. Use submatch variables $1...$n to access submatches in the resulting file path.

<DirectoryMatch pattern> ... </DirectoryMatch>
> Apply enclosed directives when filesystem directory matches *pattern*.

<FilesMatch pattern> ... </FilesMatch>
> Apply enclosed directives when file matches *pattern*.

<LocationMatch pattern> ... </LocationMatch>
> Apply enclosed directives when URL matches *pattern*.

<ProxyMatch pattern> ... </ProxyMatch>
> Apply enclosed directives when URL matches *pattern*.

Examples

Example 31. Simple match

```
# Rewrite /foo to /bar
RewriteEngine On
RewriteRule ^/foo$ /bar
```

Example 32. Match and capture group

```
# Rewrite pretty url as script parameters
RewriteRule ^/(\w+)/(\d+) /index.php?action=$1&id=$2
```

Example 33. Rewrite conditions

```
# Limit admin url to internal IP addresses
RewriteCond %{REMOTE_ADDR} !192.168.\d*.\d*
RewriteCond %{PATH_INFO}  ^admin
RewriteRule .* - [F]
```

Example 34. Redirect to SSL

```
# Make sure admin urls are served over SSL
RewriteCond   %{SERVER_PORT} !^443$
RewriteRule ^/admin/(.*)$ https://www.example.com/admin/$1
[L,R]
```

vi Editor

The *vi* program is a popular text editor on all Unix systems, and *Vim* is a popular *vi* clone with expanded regular expression support. Both use a DFA match engine. For an explanation of the rules behind a DFA engine, see "Introduction to Regexes and Pattern Matching."

Supported Metacharacters

Table 56 through Table 60 list the metacharacters and metasequences supported by *vi*. For expanded definitions of each metacharacter, see "Regex Metacharacters, Modes, and Constructs."

Table 56. vi character representation

Sequence	Meaning
Vim only	
\b	Backspace, \x08.
\e	Escape character, \x1B.

Table 56. vi character representation (continued)

Sequence	Meaning
\n	Newline, \x0A.
\r	Carriage return, \x0D.
\t	Horizontal tab, \x09.

Table 57. vi character classes and class-like constructs

Class	Meaning
[...]	Any character listed, or contained within a listed range.
[^...]	Any character that is not listed, or contained within a listed range.
[:class:]	POSIX-style character class (valid only within a character class).
.	Any character except newline (unless /s mode).
Vim only	
\w	Word character, [a-zA-z0-9_].
\W	Nonword character, [^a-zA-z0-9_].
\a	Letter character, [a-zA-z].
\A	Nonletter character, [^a-zA-z].
\h	Head of word character, [a-zA-z_].
\H	Not the head of a word character, [^a-zA-z_].
\d	Digit character, [0-9].
\D	Nondigit character, [^0-9].
\s	Whitespace character, [\t].
\S	Nonwhitespace character, [^ \t].
\x	Hex digit, [a-fA-F0-9].
\X	Nonhex digit, [^a-fA-F0-9].
\o	Octal digit, [0-7].
\O	Nonoctal digit, [^0-7].
\l	Lowercase letter, [a-z].
\L	Nonlowercase letter, [^a-z].

Table 57. vi character classes and class-like constructs (continued)

Class	Meaning
\u	Uppercase letter, [A-Z].
\U	Nonuppercase letter, [^A-Z].
\i	Identifier character defined by isident.
\I	Any nondigit identifier character.
\k	Keyword character defined by iskeyword, often set by language modes.
\K	Any nondigit keyword character.
\f	Filename character defined by isfname. Operating system-dependent.
\F	Any nondigit filename character.
\p	Printable character defined by isprint, usually x20-x7E.
\P	Any nondigit printable character.

Table 58. vi anchors and zero-width tests

Sequence	Meaning
^	Start of a line when appearing first in a regular expression; otherwise, it matches itself.
$	End of a line when appearing last in a regular expression; otherwise, it matches itself.
\<	Beginning of word boundary (i.e., a position between a punctuation or space character, and a word character).
\>	End of word boundary.

Table 59. vi mode modifiers

Modifier	Meaning
:set ic	Turn on case-insensitive mode for all searching and substitution.
:set noic	Turn off case-insensitive mode.
\u	Force next character in a replacement string to uppercase.
\l	Force next character in a replacement string to lowercase.

Table 59. vi mode modifiers (continued)

Modifier	Meaning
\U	Force all following characters in a replacement string to uppercase.
\L	Force all following characters in a replacement string to lowercase.
\E or \e	Ends a span started with \U or \L.

Table 60. vi grouping, capturing, conditional, and control

Sequence	Meaning
\(...\)	Group subpattern, and capture submatch, into \1,\2,....
\n	Contains the results of the *n*th earlier submatch. Valid in either a regex pattern, or a replacement string.
&	Evaluates to the matched text when used in a replacement string.
*	Match 0 or more times.
Vim only	
\+	Match 1 or more times.
\=	Match 1 or 0 times.
\{*n*}	Match exactly *n* times.
\{*n*,}	Match at least *n* times.
\{,*n*}	Match at most *n* times.
\{*x,y*}	Match at least *x* times, but no more than *y* times.

Pattern Matching

Searching

/pattern ?pattern

Moves to the start of the next position in the file matched by *pattern*. A *?pattern* searches backward. A search can be repeated with the n (search forward), or N (search backward) commands.

Substitution

`:[addr1[,addr2]]s/pattern/replacement/[cgp]`

Replace the text matched by *pattern* with *replacement* on every line in the address range. If no address range is given, the current line is used. Each address may be a line number, or a regular expression. If *addr1* is supplied, substitution begins on that line number (or the first matching line), and continues until the end of the file, or the line indicated (or matched) by *addr2*. There are also a number of address shortcuts, which are described in the following tables.

Substitution options

Option	Meaning
c	Prompt before each substitution.
g	Replace all matches on a line.
p	Print line after substitution.

Address shortcuts

Address	Meaning
.	Current line.
$	Last line in file.
%	Entire file.
't	Position t.
/...[/]	Next line matched by pattern.
?...[?]	Previous line matched by pattern.
\/	Next line matched by the last search.
\?	Previous line matched by the last search.
\&	Next line where the last substitution pattern matched.

Examples

Example 35. Simple search in vi

```
Find spider-man, Spider-Man, Spider Man
/[Ss]pider[- ][Mm]an
```

Example 36. Simple search in Vim

```
Find spider-man, Spider-Man, Spider Man, spiderman, SPIDER-
MAN, etc.
:set ic
/spider[- ]\=man
```

Example 37. Simple substitution in vi

```
Globally convert <br> to <br /> for XHTML compliance.
:set ic
: % s/<br>/<br \/>/g
```

Example 38. Simple substitution in Vim

```
Globally convert <br> to <br /> for XHTML compliance.
: % s/<br>/<br \/>/ig
```

Example 39. Harder substitution in Vim

```
Urlify: Turn URLs into HTML links
: % s/\(https\=:\/\/[a-z_.\\w\/\\#~:?+=&;%@!-]*\)/< a href="
\1">\1<\/a>/ic
```

Other Resources

- *Learning the vi Editor*, Sixth Edition, by Linda Lamb and Arnold Robbins (O'Reilly), is a guide to the *vi* editor and popular *vi* clones.

- *http://www.geocities.com/volontir/*, by Oleg Raisky, is an overview of *Vim* regular expression syntax.

Shell Tools

awk, *sed*, and *egrep* are a related set of Unix shell tools for text processing. *awk* uses a DFA match engine, *egrep* switches between a DFA and NFA match engine, depending on which features are being used, and *sed* uses an NFA engine. For an explanation of the rules behind these engines, see "Introduction to Regexes and Pattern Matching."

This reference covers GNU *egrep* 2.4.2, a program for searching lines of text; GNU *sed* 3.02, a tool for scripting editing commands; and GNU *awk* 3.1, a programming language for text processing.

Supported Metacharacters

awk, *egrep*, and *sed* support the metacharacters and metasequences listed in Table 61 through Table 65. For expanded definitions of each metacharacter, see "Regex Metacharacters, Modes, and Constructs."

Table 61. Shell character representations

Sequence	Meaning	Tool
\a	Alert (bell).	*awk, sed*
\b	Backspace; supported only in character class.	*awk*
\f	Form feed.	*awk, sed*
\n	Newline (line feed).	*awk, sed*
\r	Carriage return.	*awk, sed*
\t	Horizontal tab.	*awk, sed*
\v	Vertical tab.	*awk, sed*
\o*octal*	A character specified by a one-, two-, or three-digit octal code.	*sed*

Table 61. Shell character representations (continued)

Sequence	Meaning	Tool
\octal	A character specified by a one-, two-, or three-digit octal code.	*awk*
\xhex	A character specified by a two-digit hexadecimal code.	*awk, sed*
\ddecimal	A character specified by a one, two, or three decimal code.	*awk, sed*
\cchar	A named control character (e.g., \cC is Control-C).	*awk, sed*
\b	Backspace.	*awk*
\metacharacter	Escape the metacharacter, so that it literally represents itself.	*awk, sed, egrep*

Table 62. Shell character classes and class-like constructs

Class	Meaning	Tool
[...]	Matches any single character listed, or contained within a listed range.	*awk, sed, egrep*
[^...]	Matches any single character that is not listed, or contained within a listed range.	*awk, sed, egrep*
.	Matches any single character, except newline.	*awk, sed, egrep*
\w	Matches an ASCII word character, [a-zA-Z0-9_].	*egrep, sed*

Table 62. Shell character classes and class-like constructs (continued)

Class	Meaning	Tool
\W	Matches a character that is not an ASCII word character, [^a-zA-Z0-9_].	egrep, sed
[:prop:]	Matches any character in the POSIX character class.	awk, sed
[^[:prop:]]	Matches any character not in the POSIX character class.	awk, sed

Table 63. Shell anchors and other zero-width testshell tools

Sequence	Meaning	Tool
^	Matches only start of string, even if newlines are embedded.	awk, sed, egrep
$	Matches only end of search string, even if newlines are embedded.	awk, sed, egrep
\<	Matches beginning of word boundary.	egrep
\>	Matches end of word boundary.	egrep

Table 64. Shell comments and mode modifiers

Modifier	Meaning	Tool
flag: i or I	Case-insensitive matching for ASCII characters.	sed
command-line option: -i	Case-insensitive matching for ASCII characters.	egrep
set IGNORECASE to *non-zero*	Case-insensitive matching for Unicode characters.	awk

Table 65. Shell grouping, capturing, conditional, and control

Sequence	Meaning	Tool
(PATTERN)	Grouping.	*awk*
\(PATTERN\)	Group and capture submatches, filling \1, \2,...,\9.	*sed*
\n	Contains the *n*th earlier submatch.	*sed*
...|...	Alternation; match one or the other.	*egrep, awk, sed*
Greedy quantifiers		
*	Match 0 or more times.	*awk, sed, egrep*
+	Match 1 or more times.	*awk, sed, egrep*
?	Match 1 or 0 times.	*awk, sed, egrep*
\{*n*\}	Match exactly *n* times.	*sed, egrep*
\{*n*,\}	Match at least *n* times.	*sed, egrep*
\{*x,y*\}	Match at least *x* times, but no more than *y* times.	*sed, egrep*

egrep

egrep [*options*] *pattern files*

egrep searches *files* for occurrences of *pattern*, and prints out each matching line.

Example

```
$ echo 'Spiderman Menaces City!' > dailybugle.txt
$ egrep -i 'spider[- ]?man' dailybugle.txt
Spiderman Menaces City!
```

sed

sed '[*address1*][,*address2*]s/*pattern*/*replacement*/[*flags*]' *files*
sed -f *script files*

By default, *sed* applies the substitution to every line in *files*. Each address can be either a line number, or a regular expression pattern. A supplied regular expression must be defined within the forward slash delimiters (/ . . . /).

If *address1* is supplied, substitution will begin on that line number, or the first matching line, and continue until either the end of the file, or the line indicated or matched by *address2*. Two subsequences, & and \n, will be interpreted in *replacement* based on the match results.

The sequence & is replaced with the text matched by *pattern*. The sequence \n corresponds to a capture group (1...9) in the current match. Here are the available flags:

n

> Substitute the *n*th match in a line, where *n* is between 1 and 512.

g

> Substitute all occurrences of *pattern* in a line.

p

> Print lines with successful substitutions.

w *file*
> Write lines with successful substitutions to *file*.

Example

Change date formats from *MM/DD/YYYY* to *DD.MM.YYYY*.

```
$ echo 12/30/1969' |
 sed 's!\([0-9][0-9]\)/\([0-9][0-9]\)/\([0-9]\{2,4\}\)!
\2.\1.\3!g'
```

---

awk

awk '*instructions*' *files*
awk -f *script files*

The *awk* script contained in *instructions* or *script* should be a series of /*pattern*/ {*action*} pairs. The *action* code is applied to each line matched by *pattern*. *awk* also supplies several functions for pattern matching.

Functions

match(*text, pattern*)
> If *pattern* matches in *text*, return the position in *text* where the match starts. A failed match returns zero. A successful match also sets the variable RSTART to the position where the match started, and the variable RLENGTH to the number of characters in the match.

---

gsub(*pattern*, *replacement*, *text*)

> Substitute each match of *pattern* in *text* with *replacement*, and return the number of substitutions. Defaults to $0 if *text* is not supplied.

sub(*pattern*, *replacement*, *text*)

> Substitute first match of *pattern* in *text* with *replacement*. A successful substitution returns 1, and an unsuccessful substitution returns 0. Defaults to $0 if *text* is not supplied.

Example

Create an *awk* file and then run it from the command line.

```
$ cat sub.awk
{
    gsub(/https?:\/\/[a-z_.\\w\/\\#~:?+=&;%@!-]*/,
                   "<a href=\"\&\">\&</a>");

    print
}

$ echo "Check the web site, http://www.oreilly.com/
catalog/repr" | awk -f sub.awk
```

Other Resources

- *sed and awk*, by Dale Dougherty and Arnold Robbins (O'Reilly), is an introduction and reference to both tools.

Index

We'd like to hear your suggestions for improving our indexes. Send email to *index@oreilly.com*.